SOCIAL CAPITAL AND LIFELONG LEARNING

John Field

First published in Great Britain in June 2005 by

The Policy Press
University of Bristol
Fourth Floor
Beacon House
Queen's Road
Bristol BS8 1QU
UK

Tel +44 (0)117 331 4054
Fax +44 (0)117 331 4093
e-mail tpp-info@bristol.ac.uk
www.policypress.org.uk

British Library Cataloguing in Publication Data
A catalogue record for this book is available from the British Library.

Library of Congress Cataloging-in-Publication Data
A catalog record for this book has been requested.

ISBN 1 86134 655 7 paperback

A hardcover version of this book is also available

Cover design by Qube Design Associates, Bristol.
Front cover: photograph supplied by kind permission of www.third-avenue.co.uk
Printed and bound in Great Britain by Hobbs the Printers Ltd, Southampton.

Contents

List of tables and figures

Tables

Figures

Acknowledgements

Gordon Burn's bittersweet novel, *The North of England Home Service*, revolves around the life of Ray Cruddas, an aging light entertainer who now runs a club in a post-industrial city in the north-east of England. The club is a commercial caricature of the past, where men come dressed in flat caps and mufflers, women in shawls and curlers, to dine and dance among washtubs and mangles, "...content to be cast back to a time when nobody spoke of 'community' and everybody belonged to one" (Burn, 2003, p 71). This is a fine dismissal of a particular discourse of community. Yet Burn also shows how Cruddas is sustained by friends and connections, from the people he sees sporadically around a tea van to an elderly ex-boxer who gives his life meaning through the friendship. Furthermore, given what we know about the negative consequences of loneliness and isolation, maybe the idea of rebuilding community is not so foolish after all.

Much of the data on which this book rests was generated by, or with, other people. It originated in a project funded under the Economic and Social Research Council's Learning Society Programme. Lynda Spence worked with me on the Northern Ireland fieldwork; Tom Schuller co-directed the project and worked on its Scottish dimension and, although I do not use his data, I was much influenced by his analytical thinking. Some of the quantitative data comes from the Northern Ireland Life and Times Survey; Ann Marie Gray of the University of Ulster and Paula Devine of Queen's University, Belfast, who invited me to contribute to the design of a lifelong learning module in the Survey, also allowed me access to the findings and arranged a seminar to share and debate the findings. I wish to thank Fiona Aldridge, Naomi Sargant and Alan Tuckett of the National Institute of Adult Continuing Education, who invited me to assist in the annual adult learning survey for 2002, allowed me to access the findings and provided opportunities for discussion of their importance.

My thinking has benefited from countless discussions at seminars and conferences. The Scottish Adult Learning Partnership's seminar on community-based adult learning and social capital, held in Edinburgh in November 2004, caused me to rethink much of Chapter Five. I have also learned from the online debates arranged by the Observatory on Place Management, Social Capital and Learning (www.obs-pascal.com). Above all, I have benefited over several years from the highly congenial meetings of the Active Democratic Citizenship network of the European Society for Research in the Education of Adults. Finally, as befits the topic of this volume, I have learned a great deal from countless informal encounters and exchanges with friends and colleagues, at Stirling and elsewhere. As ever, though, any weaknesses and errors are my fault alone.

learning is in itself a challenging idea, and not one that is easily absorbed by more conventional education and training systems. However, the idea of a learning society also raises yet more radical, complicated and (I believe) interesting issues, which form the heart of this book. At their core is the question of whether some social arrangements might be better at promoting the acquisition of new skills and knowledge than others. Are there social values, and patterns of behaviour, that discourage us from getting the most out of education and training, not only as children but also in our adult lives? Are we more likely to learn and apply and create new knowledge in some types of social circumstances than others? Do we learn more, and more valuably, from our social connections than from educational institutions? Are there types of relationship that inhibit us from learning and creating knowledge, while others promote it? And if any of this holds water, then what might we – policy makers, educationalists and the wider community – do about it?

This is a very broad view of the learning society, and it takes us into largely uncharted territory. It rests, of course, on existing debates about the nature and scope of human learning. In particular, it shifts attention away from the conventional focus of educational theory and debate, which is on the formal instruction that takes place in designated institutions such as schools or colleges. It also takes a view of humans as being always both acquirers/transmitters of existing knowledge and creators of new knowledge. In both capacities – acquirers/transmitters and constructors of knowledge – people find themselves benefiting from and constrained by social structures, practices and institutions. Yet at the same time, people are constantly creating and recreating the structures, institutions and practices in which they find themselves; moreover, they constantly use and apply and create new information and understandings in their reshaping of social arrangements. While much of this process of change may be rather mundane in itself – buying something to wear, leaving a partner, finding another job, arguing with a parent – such everyday changes add up to a wider process of social transformation.

Sociologists and educationists will recognise where this line of argument comes from. Educationalists will spot that my view of learning is broadly a constructivist one, which recognises the ways in which people are constantly and actively engaged in creating meaning and new understandings as they go through their everyday lives. Sociologists will know that my account of the interplay between people and social arrangements is part of a long tradition of interpretative thinking about structure and agency, and is partly influenced by Pierre Bourdieu's sociology of class and power (Bourdieu, 1977), Anthony Giddens' theory of structuration (1984), and the more recent work of Giddens (1991) and

Introduction

During the 1990s, a widespread debate opened over the idea and goal of a 'learning society'. This debate was bound up with ideas for modernising and reforming education and training systems, so that they not only ensured that young people were able to enter adult life with a robust platform of skills and knowledge, but also that adults themselves were able to continue their learning throughout their lifespan. At its narrowest, this simply involved the adjustment of existing systems and institutions so that they could better promote achievement and participation, particularly among the new cadres of highly skilled knowledge workers. A learning society is the precondition, it is said, of a high performance knowledge economy. Other, more generous visions of the learning society have emphasised the value of learning both in its own right and as a gateway to participation and full citizenship: a civilised society, in this view, is one that provides opportunities for learning for all, regardless of their age or life stage, as a right.

Even if we take a comparatively narrow definition of the learning society, the implications are radical. Even if limited to the formal arrangements by which any community ensures that its members gain the skills and knowledge required in and for a rapidly changing economy, this perspective has already generated considerable impetus for reform of education and training systems. Staid policy makers meeting in sober international governmental agencies like the European Union or the Organisation for Economic Co-operation and Development are concluding that the new economy demands a dramatically different education and training system from the one that exists today. In a 1994 White Paper on economic competitiveness and growth, the European Commission went so far as to call for future educational reform initiatives to be based "on the concept of developing, generalising and systematising lifelong learning and continuing training" (CEC, 1994, p 136). This is a radical ambition indeed which has led the Commission and many economically advanced natior to turn their attention to lifewide as well as lifelong learning: that is, to tl many different areas of life in which people continue to acquire a create new skills and knowledge throughout their lifespan. In pract terms, this has led to an interest in such areas as workplace learning, fa learning and community learning, and in how they can be related to in a telling word, 'captured' for – more formal systems for recog knowledge and competences.

Recognition of the complexity and diffusion of lifelong and l

Ulrich Beck (2000) on what is often called 'reflexive modernisation'. These are the footprints that will be seen by my fellow academics; I hope that other readers might agree to forgive this paragraph as a brief scholarly aside. The point I am trying to make boils down to this: the concept of learning is very different from the concept of education, and people's active engagement in the wider social context is an extremely important aspect of the distinction between the two.

This fundamental dissimilarity is all too often downplayed or even ignored. While formal instruction is of considerable importance, both to individuals and to the wider community, it has to be set in the wider perspective of the infinite variety and range of different kinds of learning that people undertake. Much education is experienced as an external imposition, something that is a formal requirement, and much of whose content passes us by. Learning is a much more ubiquitous process by which individuals and communities actively seek to add to their capacity for attaining their goals. It happens in a wide variety of settings, and across different areas of our lives. Only some of our learning takes place in educational settings, and even then what we learn is not necessarily what the teachers intend: at school we might learn how to deal with bullies, how to dispose of unwanted school dinners, or how to avoid the rules on chewing gum and mobile phones. All this happens alongside our success or failure in mastering French, memorising dates and conducting mildly amusing chemistry experiments. Learning is a fearsomely broad concept, with famously blurred boundaries: it is the active process by which we engage with our changing environment and try to take control of our lives.

Such distinctions have been bread and butter in the adult education world for at least 50 years. Many adult educators have tended to draw a clear contrast between formal learning (planned and organised instruction in designated institutions) on the one hand, and non-formal and informal learning on the other (see Colley et al, 2003). The term 'non-formal learning' has usually been used to describe the education that is provided by bodies whose main purpose is something other than education, such as trades unions, voluntary associations and companies, to give but three examples. The term 'informal learning' is a very wide one, which can refer to all those forms of learning that take place as a result of an individual's life experiences, rather than as a result of any intentional instruction by a third party. This encompasses a broad range from incidental learning, which is simply a by-product of experience, to a more determined attempt by someone to teach themselves by such means as visiting a library, seeking advice or surfing the Internet. Such attempts at definitional clarity are doomed to fail, given the all-encompassing nature of learning as a process.

Furthermore, many writers in the adult education tradition have tended not simply to distinguish between these broad types of learning, but to see them in a rather simplistic manner as directly opposed to one another; in fact, they are far more likely to be intermingled and to occur simultaneously alongside one another, in complex and hard-to-capture ways (Colley et al, 2003).

In addition to these different ways of analysing learning, we may also distinguish between different types of knowledge. Once more, the language of the learning society is linked with a shift away from the customary focus on formal and certificated bodies of explicit and codified knowledge of the type tested in the examinations system. Educationalists increasingly recognise the importance of tacit knowledge, often embedded in people's activities and relationships, of a kind that cannot easily be articulated and made explicit (Polanyi, 1966). Perhaps the most widely known analysis of this issue is the distinction between types of knowledge that was made in the 1990s by Michael Gibbon and his collaborators (Gibbon et al, 1994). These authors draw a contrast between Mode 1 knowledge, which they describe as academic, rooted in single disciplines and based on abstract and codified generalisations, and Mode 2 knowledge, which they see as hybridised, created by teams from different disciplines and different sectors, generated by practical problems and capable of application, and often highly specific to certain contexts. They believe that, while Mode 1 knowledge might continue to be important for the foreseeable future, Mode 2 is increasingly coming to dominate the new world of scientific production. Moreover, this is a form of knowledge that, these authors emphasise, is created by and through groups rather than by isolated individuals; its origin lies in collective attempts to solve problems, and its meaning is only realised through application in an organisational setting.

The central argument of this book is that people's social relationships play a vital part in their capacity for learning. I see this proposition as holding good whether we understand learning as simply concerned with the acquisition of skills and knowledge or, more generously, as also concerned with their creation. This should not really be a surprising argument: after all, we are all affected by the attitudes of those whom we like and trust, and there is no obvious reason why this should not be just as true for skills and knowledge as any other area of life. Indeed, this claim is reasonably well established in respect of young people, and it would be hard to find an educationalist who denies that family and peer group help to shape attitudes towards school and college. Albeit in a rather limited sense, then, the idea that social networks shape educational achievement among the young is widely accepted.

The lines of this argument with respect to young people are fairly straightforward. If our friends and family admire academic achievement, then we are likely to share this outlook and will try to bring up our children accordingly. If we are surrounded by people who take pride in high quality craft skills, we are more likely to think of placing our children in an apprenticeship. This is not always such a straightforward relationship, as the case of migrant communities suggests. If newcomer communities view the schools system as alien and oppressive, then they may be inclined to be suspicious of academic achievement within that system. Newcomers who see schooling as a means of overcoming economic disadvantage and social prejudice within the host society are more likely to place pressure on young people to achieve within the terms of that system. Yet, even if the picture is a complex one, it is widely agreed that people's connections shape the educational experiences of the young. This book sets out to explore the possibility that social relationships can also affect the lifelong and lifewide learning undertaken by adults.

In this analysis, I make considerable use of the growing debate over social capital (Field, 2003a). Social capital may be defined as consisting of "social networks, the reciprocities that arise from them, and the value of these for achieving mutual goals" (Schuller et al, 2000, p 1). The concept is an increasingly familiar one in the social sciences, and it has been particularly influential in the study of such areas as school attainment, business innovation, community development and social inclusion. The notion emphasises the important role that people's relationships, and the values that they share with their connections, play in enabling them to cooperate for mutual advantage. Of course, this is hardly a new idea: most people have noticed the way that connections – family, friends, even casual acquaintances and friends-of-friends – will help one another out. The late 19th-century scholar, Emile Durkheim, often praised as a founding father of sociology, believed that the complex multitude of connections between individuals helped to ensure that society was held together through what he called 'organic solidarity', which he contrasted with the habitual and heirarchical 'mechanical solidarity' of the feudal order (Durkheim, 1933). At a more common-sense level, people can often be heard to claim that: "It isn't what you know that counts, it's who you know" – a phrase usually used to explain the otherwise inexplicable success of a particularly talentless individual. Yet, if the core ideas behind the theory of social capital are well known, the current debate does mark a new departure, in several ways. Three are especially relevant for this book.

First and foremost, the concept of social capital is concerned with power. By treating social relationships as a form of capital, it proposes that they are a resource, which people can then draw on to achieve their goals. The fact that social capital is a resource that empowers people does not necessarily mean that everyone with some friends will therefore exercise power over everybody else. People can use their connections to exert power over others, but they can also use their connections to exert power with others. Like some of the authors whose ideas I explore in Chapter One, I see social capital as one among many sets of possible resources. Pierre Bourdieu, the French social theorist and anthropologist, defined social capital as one of a number of significant sets of resources, which included cultural capital (the ability to use cultural markers such as taste as a way of asserting distinctiveness and superiority) as well as economic capital. Bourdieu thought that social capital was almost invariably less important than economic capital, and this is a view that I am inclined to share. The key issue here is that social capital serves as one possible resource that can increase people's capacity for achieving their goals by securing the cooperation of others.

A considerable amount of the attention paid to social capital concerns its relationship with education and related issues. I explore this literature in Chapter Two. Following James Coleman's pioneering studies of the impact of social capital on schoolchildren's attainment, much of this literature has concentrated on schooling. In so far as educational researchers have explored social capital and learning outside schools, their focus has remained largely institutional, with a growing number of studies of higher education and other establishments of post-compulsory education and training. Informal learning, by contrast, has received scant attention from educational researchers, and Chapter Two examines empirical evidence on the connection between people's networks and both their informal and formal learning. Chapter Three then considers the issue of values and behaviour, based on survey data on people's attitudes towards learning and the way that these can be related to their engagement in wider sets of social relationship.

The empirical evidence suggests that there are highly significant links between people's networks and their learning. Yet, although they are significant, these links are neither simple nor do they act independently of a range of other factors. This has a wider significance beyond that of education and training alone, for there is a burgeoning interest among business researchers in the way that social capital can influence organisational performance by facilitating – or impeding – the flow of knowledge and information within and between firms. In addition, there is a smaller but still significant body of work on the relevance of community-based social capital for the well-being and economy of particular neighbourhoods and regions. The extent to which the concept of social capital can itself act as a bridge between different disciplines and diverse fields of study is a strong reason why it is worth closer investigation in the context of lifelong learning. However, given the significance of learning for our understanding of changing patterns of social behaviour in contemporary societies, the empirical data also have a wider theoretical significance. I attempt to grapple with this in Chapter Four.

The concept of social capital has shown considerable potential as a way of enabling dialogue between academics and a range of different stakeholders. It has caused quite a lot of excitement among academics, mainly in sociology, but also in political studies and economics, as well as in applied fields such as health studies, criminology, management, media studies and education. However, there has also been strong interest in the potential application of the concept to policy development. Among the peak international governmental bodies, important work on social capital has appeared from the World Bank, the Organisation for Economic Co-operation and Development, and – if to a lesser extent – the European Commission. This work is discussed further in Chapter Five, which also looks at the ways in which policy makers and their advisers have tried to work with the idea of social capital. Policy interest in social capital almost invariably leads to a concern for the implications for learning (usually conceptualised as human capital), whether seen as an outcome of social capital or as a source of it.

Since I am asking questions about the concept of social capital, while simultaneously making use of it, it is appropriate to add a few words about terminology. Language is important: calling something capital makes a difference. In part, this is because the language of economics lends itself to policy making, which is always interested in identifying and justifying priorities for public investment. Where ideas such as 'community' or 'lifelong learning' sound fluffy and possibly wasteful, the language of human capital and social capital suggests that we can identify and measure the costs and benefits of public investments in each, and compare them with similar counts for other areas of public spending. Equally, those who wish to attract the attention of policy makers to their claims may believe that they are more likely to get a favourable hearing if they write and speak in the language of the merchant banker. The socialist economist, Bob Fine, has rejected the concept of social capital for precisely this reason: for him, this language represents the colonising drive of economics as a discipline, and the Treasury as the dominant government ministry (Fine, 2000). Well, perhaps so, but we might equally see things the other way round.

The multiplication of capitals – among them social capital, cultural capital, identity capital and intellectual capital – point just as much to what we might describe as a societalisation of economic thinking as to the reverse. Traditional free market economics, with its atomised view of individuals' preferences and interests, has given way to a perspective that recognises the social and cultural dimensions of human behaviour. For policy makers, this means that even purely economic policy measures have to take account of the wider social relationships and values that shape people's behaviour, and determine how they will receive and respond to new policies. This is above all the case in an area such as lifelong learning, where the policy interventions rely entirely on individuals' and organisations' consent if they are to have any impact – and where the absence of consent will produce dramatic negative consequences.

Much recent debate has focused on the twin issues of social capital and lifelong learning, and increasingly it is concerned to examine the relationships between them. This issue is of interest to social scientists, not least because it connects to current debates about reflexivity, identity and change. It also has implications for practice, and even perhaps for policy. If somewhat hesitantly, some significant sections of the policy community are open to persuasion on the relevance of this debate for their concerns. At present, this discussion is in an early stage and, if nothing else, this book sets out to provide a rather firmer basis for further research and analysis.

ONE

Social connections and lifelong learning

Much of our life is passed in the company of others. As well as our loved ones, we routinely encounter a cast of people whom we know, including workmates, friends, neighbours, business associates, shop assistants, bartenders, club members and the postman or woman. As we go through life, so we acquire new relationships and lose old ones; and the meanings of relationships can often change over time. This book examines the ways in which our everyday relationships, and the patterns that they assume, affect our capacity to learn across the lifespan.

Some people, of course, have a wider range of relationships than others, and some have closer relationships than others. Whatever the nature of our relationships, though, all of us use them on a regular basis. They help us secure goods and services; they provide opportunities to chat about common interests and hear the latest gossip; they underpin our sense of who we are; and – we hope – they give us affection, as well as giving us an object for affection. Conversely, people who are isolated are likely to suffer from their lack of connections. It is not just that, to state the obvious, most people think that loneliness feels unpleasant. Isolation also means that there is no one to turn to when the going gets tough, no one to borrow things from, no one to let you know what is going on – nor anyone for whom you can provide similar services in return.

This book is centrally concerned with the way that our relationships are also a resource, and serve as a form of capital. In particular, it looks at the way that this social capital can influence the way in which people acquire new skills, information and ideas throughout their lifespan, and in turn create new skills, meanings and knowledge. Both social capital and lifelong learning have attracted considerable analytical attention in recent years. This chapter seeks to explore both sets of ideas, and examine the relationship between them. It does so in the context of the idea of the learning society, along with related notions such as the learning region, the learning city and the learning organisation. What all these ideas share is the belief that the architecture of people's relationships with one another, and the quality of the learning they undertake, are fundamentally linked, and that the two can be harnessed to one another in a mutually beneficial manner.

Most authors also recognise that these are complex issues, and that there are few quick and simple lessons for policy makers (Smith and Spurling, 1999; NESF, 2003; Faris, 2004). A degree of conceptual clarity is one prerequisite of analysis. This opening chapter suggests that we need a differentiated conception of social capital, which recognises that people are involved in different kinds of connections with one another, and that these various connections may therefore provide access to widely differing types and levels of resources. It also argues for a differentiated concept of lifelong learning, which acknowledges that learning brings about continuing tensions between emancipation and subjection.

Unlike most earlier studies of networks and learning, this study mostly concentrates on the relationship between social capital and learning in adult life. This chapter provides a conceptual background to the more grounded chapters that follow. It starts with an account of current debates over the social contexts of adult learning. This leads into a brief consideration of the long association between civic engagement and adult learning – an association that now appears to be at an end, and is increasingly being displaced by a very different relationship between people's adult learning and their social ties. It then moves on to expound the concept of social capital, which has developed rapidly across the social sciences. It then examines the ways in which social capital and adult learning might be related to one another, and concludes by sketching out a hypothetical taxonomy of possible relationships.

Adult learning in its social context

People's learning always takes place in a wider social context. Until recently, relatively little was known about how that social context was related to the learning that people undertake in adult life. In particular, there have been few attempts to examine the relationship between adult learning and what we might call the meso level of people's institutional affiliations, and their involvement in a range of associations from the family to civic movements of various kinds. At the macro level, research into the social context of participation has been limited to a broad recognition that such general social factors as socioeconomic status, ethnicity and gender appear to play a powerful role in determining people's opportunities and shaping their decisions (for example, Sargant, 1997). If large-scale surveys tell us about the wider statistical trends, studies influenced by situated learning and experiential learning have tended to emphasise the immediate environment of the learning situation (Lave and Wenger, 1991), while life history researchers generally explore the subjective experiences and perceptions of individuals (West, 1996; Merrill, 1999). While these studies have shed a great deal of light on what we might call both the macro and micro levels of adult learning, they generally fail to acknowledge the immediate patterns of social interaction and association within which individuals' immediate learning environments are embedded.

Yet this is far from being virgin territory. If there has been only limited attention to the way that learning is embedded in everyday social life (Fordham et al, 1979; Jarvis, 1987), the relationship between active citizenship and adult learning has been a common theme in the scholarly literature (Bron, 1995). European historians have been particularly interested in the role of popular social movements in providing and demanding adult education, a role which was particularly strong between the 19th and early 20th centuries (see, for example, Goldman, 1995; Fieldhouse, 1996; Rose, 2002; Roberts 2003). In Britain and Scandinavia, the roots of such educative movements can be found in the later 18th century in the free churches; in Scandinavia, and in parts of Britain and Ireland, this was subsequently accompanied by the growth of temperance movements. With the onset of industrialisation and mass urbanisation, the main 19th- and 20th-century European labour movements were also greatly exercised with the role of education in empowering their followers. Even in the present century, workers' parades in many nations are led by colourful banners proclaiming that "Knowledge is Power" (Gorman, 1986), a view that was expressed in 20th-century Britain through such diverse organisations as the Labour Colleges, the Workers' Educational Association (WEA) and Ruskin College. While the women's movement has received somewhat less scholarly attention, it was equally concerned with the education of its members, not least in order to demonstrate that they were culturally equipped for, as well as morally deserving of, the right to vote. By the time that the Women's Institutes were launched in 1917 to provide adult education for country women, the much less well-known Cooperative Women's Guild had already been doing the same for working-class women for three decades.

Agnieszka Bron describes these movements as "schools for democracy", training their members in the principles of civic association while offering a more general education to underpin their claim for citizenship (Bron, 1995, p 21). In a 1957 address to the University of London's extra-mural department, R.H. Tawney suggested that this organic connection was not coincidental, but rather that educational depth was itself a direct result of the alternative conception of society that social movements embodied:

> All serious educational movements have, in England, been also social movements. They have been the expression in one sphere – the training of mind and character – of some distinctive

> conception of the life proper to man and the kind of society in which he can best live it. (Tawney, 1964, p 84)

Forget, at least for a moment, some of the boundaries of Tawney's language (we are less likely today to think that a world made up of Englishmen may stand for a wider social truth). Much more importantly for the argument of this book, Tawney's 'classical' era of adult education for citizenship is now at an end. In western Europe and Australasia, adult education movements developed from the 1920s onwards that were less concerned with democratic citizenship and collective advance than with leisure and sociability. Inevitably, this also affected those adult education movements that had been established to promote political and social change. If anything, it was accelerated following the creation of a growing welfare state – something that many of the major social movements had worked towards, and whose achievement they hailed as a landmark in the twin processes of modernisation and democratisation.

By the 1980s and 1990s, the social movements that had created modern adult education institutions were facing a long-term decline in support. Trades unions, social democratic parties and cooperative associations fought falling levels of membership, and even more rapidly tumbling levels of member involvement; empty chapels were converted into shops and housing; newer social movements had appeared on the scene, such as the feminist and peace movements or the anti-globalisation campaign, only to vanish with equal rapidity. Meanwhile, social purpose adult education had become a minority tradition, tolerated but clearly marginal to a system of provision that was increasingly instrumental and vocational or consumerist in character. In so far as the newer social movements were also learning movements, in Tawney's sense, they have limited interest in the creation of relationships with formal adult education institutions.

Nevertheless, many European researchers have continued to examine the ways in which adult learning intersects with civic engagement in contemporary society (Hedoux, 1982; Elsdon et al, 1995; Brandstetter and Kellner, 2001; Schemmann and Bron, 2001; Coare and Johnston, 2003). Empirically, too, there is compelling evidence to suggest that those people who are involved in the public sphere are also likely to be actively learning something. This was already clear in the 1960s from the findings of what became the first of many large-scale surveys of adult learning in England and Wales. Undertaken in 1969 by the National Institute of Adult Education, the study found that people studying either in local authority or WEA/university adult education programmes were far more likely to belong to clubs and societies, and to take an active interest in community service and cultural pursuits. The same study also found a significant difference between the two groups of adult education students, with the local authority students showing higher levels of sociability and engagement than the population at large, but with even higher levels among those who were taking WEA/university courses (NIAE, 1970, pp 145-8). A systematic survey of British providers a decade later led its authors to conclude that: "The tradition of the political relevance of adult education is alive but not well. A good deal is going on but it is small compared with total activity, and there is a lack of philosophy and rationale" (Groombridge et al, 1982, p 15).

Yet, it never occurred to the authors to question the assumption that adult education and civic engagement should have a relationship.

Such certainty about the desirability of an explicit link between adult education and participation did not, in Britain, survive the 1980s. Nevertheless, a number of more recent studies have confirmed that people who are active citizens also tend to be lifelong learners (Field, 1991; Benn, 1996, 2000; Preston, 2003), even though the two sets of activities might be thought to compete for people's time. There is evidence, for instance, that workers who belong to a trades union, all other things being equal, are more likely than non-members to take up job-related training (Livingstone and Sawchuk, 2004; TUC, 2004). Survey data have shown that adults who take part in various organised cultural activities are more likely to take part in learning (Sargant, 1997, ch 11; Field, 2003b). While these studies have not been able to identify which is cause and which is effect, they do tend repeatedly to confirm the existence of a strong association between civic engagement and adult learning.

Much research finds that those with the highest levels of formal education are more likely to be involved in civic activity (Field, 2003a, pp 75-6). As already noted, disentangling cause and effect is difficult. Yet, here there is some evidence of causality, particularly with respect to the effects of higher education participation on the attitudes and behaviour of graduates. One analysis using data from the British Household Panel Study showed that, while there were already higher levels of civic activity among those who planned to enter higher education than those who did not, actual participation had a very small additional effect both for young and mature students (Egerton, 2002; see also Emler and McNamara, 1996). So, it may well be that, for many people, civic engagement and educational participation form closely related but distinct elements in a common way of life; as Bourdieu might put it, they are parts of an educated, middle-class habitus.

As well as the evidence linking learning and sociability in the civic arena, both are also said to have direct economic consequences. Scholars interested in business innovation and technological change, for instance, are increasingly attending to the ways in which people's relationships are intertwined with their learning. Rather than presenting change as the achievement of heroic individuals – be they inventors or entrepreneurs – knowledge-based innovation is increasingly seen as part of a process of problem solving that is rooted in social networks and collaborative learning (Porter, 1990; Lundvall and Johnson, 1994; Lall, 2000; Maskell, 2000; Szreter, 2000; Cooke, 2002).

According to these authors, the spread of new techniques and approaches is in large measure a product of the range and nature of entrepreneurs' relationships, and the learning that these enable. Lundvall and Johnson (1994), in particular, have emphasised the way in which collective learning by firms benefits from what they define as localised systems of innovation. Even when competing with other companies in a globalised market place, firms benefit from access to information and ideas from other insiders whom they meet on a face-to-face basis (see also Maskell, 2000; Maskell et al, 1998).Given that people working in the same industry tend to hold shared assumptions and common practices, and sometimes use a specialised language full of references and allusions that are obscure to outsiders, localised networks particularly facilitate access to tacit and embedded forms of knowledge. Polanyi (1966) coined the term 'tacit knowledge' to describe knowledge that is embodied through practice, and bedded into specific relationships and contexts. While its results can be seen in the outcomes of action, in contrast with codified knowledge, tacit knowledge itself cannot readily be made explicit and articulated in a codifiable form.

In practice, the boundaries between tacit and explicit knowledge are often blurred. In a study of informal learning among software engineers, Juani Swart and Nicholas Kinnie found that many of their respondents found it impossible to write down or codify their technical knowledge; even though they were familiar with a particular software code, they could teach it only through shared practice (Swart and Kinnie, 2003, p 63). The key point is that tacit knowledge in particular appears to be created on a shared basis, and transmitted most efficiently where people know, and trust, one another. More explicit and abstract forms of knowledge, by contrast, can be generated in one space and then passed on to others in codified and often formulaic forms.

Social capital and trust appear, then, to play a highly significant role in underpinning innovation by promoting informal learning. However, Lundvall and Johnson also note the important part played by external sources of knowledge (such as universities) in localised systems of innovation, and they predict that the more sustained and intensive the interactions, the more likely it is that new information will be taken up and applied (Lundvall and Johnson, 1994). As one recent authoritative review of industry/university collaboration in Britain put it, the current consensus is that: "The best forms of knowledge transfer involve human interaction" (Lambert, 2003, p 31).

Nor is the economic significance of social capital confined to the behaviour of entrepreneurs and business leaders. Much the same can also be said about the role of social connections within the wider workplace in enabling cooperation. This is hardly new: informal interaction among workers has always been important. For as long as waged labour has existed, workers have used their own and others' personal acquaintances to help find jobs for themselves and for their children (usually sons), to pass on skills and knowledge related to their job, to equip themselves to organise and resist demands from their employers, and generally to figure out how to make life more bearable. Although the bureaucratic structures of the welfare state and Fordist organisation of industry were partly adopted precisely because they provided alternatives to these informal networks, in practice people continued to rely on connections to get by. Granovetter's classical paper on the important role played by loose ties in finding work, for instance, was published in the early 1970s, when Fordist manufacturing was still in its heyday (Granovetter, 1973). Structural changes in the economy, rather than eroding the value of personal connections, are instead making them more significant. Just to cite one example, government-sponsored skills surveys typically identify so-called 'soft skills' like interpersonal communications, team working, problem solving and customer relations as among the "skills most commonly found lacking" in job seekers (Scottish Enterprise, 2003, p 35; see also Expert Group on Future Skills Needs, 2003, pp 86-94).

Recent developments in the organisation of work put even more weight on the ways in which different types of workers create and exchange knowledge. In a recent analysis, Yrjo Engeström has explored the learning required in and generated by what he calls 'co-configuration' – that is, types of work that create products or services that can be adapted by the user (or will adapt themselves) *after* they have been sold. Engeström sees co-configuration as typically found in jobs that involve integrated combinations of products and services, such as medical care, where the user is one of a number of partners who must engage in continuing dialogue with a variety of different producers (Engeström, 2004, pp 11-13).

In a globalised and highly networked economy, it might be asked precisely why face-to-face encounters apparently still play such a decisive role in business success. Part of the answer appears to lie in the way in which social connections help to generate trust between people, and thereby foster the exchange of information and ideas. In an important historical study, Simon Szreter has persuasively argued that far more attention should be paid to the way in which people's networks give them access to information (Szreter, 2000). For Szreter, the crucial issue is the way in which "individuals' capacities to process information are distributed across an economy" (Szreter, 2000, p 61). Social capital, he suggests, can be seen as minimising the transaction costs of passing information between different economic actors. The example that he provides is the experience of buying a car: dealers make many claims and provide a great deal of information, but a purchaser still needs to spend time finding out whether the deal is a good one or not. We might go slightly further than Szreter, and suggest that people's networks are not only useful in passing information across the economy; they also help people form judgements about competing claims, and provide guidance on the application of new information across a variety of contexts.

People's social connections, then, have value in a number of different areas of their lives. There appears, first, to be a clear, positive association between civic engagement and adult learning. This has helped create a consensus among scholars and other commentators on what many clearly see as a beneficial cycle of civic engagement and adult learning (Elsdon et al, 1995; Coare and Johnston, 2003; Preston, 2003). It is widely agreed that those people who are most engaged are also the most likely to undertake learning; and, equally, it is generally accepted that those who are most active as learners in adult life are also prone to become involved in civic activity. In so far as both these activities are viewed as desirable in themselves, then they can be seen as helping to create a virtuous cycle. However, they also appear to have further consequences, as in the case of business innovation, which are also positive.

One obvious conclusion, then, might be that strengthening our communities is a simple way to promote more effective learning, and vice versa. Yet, this is a rather rose-tinted picture, and it leaves out the disruptive effects of many wider social trends. Some very popular newspapers, for example, appear to lament on a daily basis the way in which modern society is falling apart. The rise of communitarian ideas in the 1990s was a very real response to widely shared fears over the collapse of civic values. Communitarian writers like Etzioni emphasised family, wider kinship circles and neighbourliness as a source of social justice, self-reliance and mutual aid – in short, as the basis of civic virtue (Etzioni, 1995).

Many might criticise communitarians for their somewhat outmoded emphasis on social arrangements – such as the nuclear family – that cannot simply be rebuilt by an act of will, and which are moreover highly contested. However, if communitarianism seems somewhat conservative, much academic and policy thinking about community building is informed by similar beliefs in a link between community building and social inclusion (Jarvie, 2003). Such beliefs can also be found in thinking about adult learning, among both practitioners and academics. Ken Robinson, for example, has argued that so-called 'soft skills' are in decline among the young precisely because of the collapse of community. According to Robinson, contemporary students spend more and more time concentrating on desk work and terminals, and less time socialising; their parents spend less time talking to their youngsters; and fear of crime together with the availability of home-based entertainments mean that young people are less likely to spend time playing and communicating with one another (Robinson, 2001, p 140). So, it is worth exploring some of the basic communitarian assumptions about the decay of community in contemporary societies.

First, there is indeed an observable tendency for fixed social coordinates – including our relationships with other people – to be replaced by a more open and fluid range of indicators. Our ties with other people are not fixed once and for all, even when those ties are extremely intimate, but are increasingly shaped and held together (or abandoned) as a result of our own and other people's choices. Rather than seeking to restore bonds based on habit and tradition, it seems more sensible to recognise that people's social ties no longer offer the kind of basis for longer-term social stability that they did when they were habitual and unquestioned. Thus the Catalan sociologist, Manuel Castells, speaks of the rise of a network society, where fixed and direct relationships of all kinds are being replaced by open systems of coordination, based on what he calls "networks of networks" (Castells, 1996). Ulrich Beck adopts a rather different perspective, arguing that we live in an age characterised by risks that are of human creation, where the ethic of "individual self-fulfilment and achievement is the most powerful current in modern society" (Beck, 2000, p 165). For Beck, the sources of collective identity and meaning that used to underpin the western industrial democracies – family, national state, ethnicity, class and job – are exhausted and no longer provide for either personal security or social integration (Beck, 1992).

This is exactly where the current debate over social capital comes in, rooted as it is in accounts of change and transformation in the nature of community. Of course, as will be shown later, there is disagreement about the precise components of social capital, at least among those who have dominated the debate so far. Yet, whether we focus on family ties, neighbourhood connections or participation in social movements and voluntary associations, it is impossible to ignore the evidence of change over time. Beck perhaps exaggerates when he suggests that these changes amount simply to by-products of the growth of individualism and the individualisation of social relations (Beck, 2000). Yet, he and Anthony Giddens are surely right to discern an uncoupling of social life from habitual sources of meaning and unthinking obligation, and a corresponding shift towards the continuing refashioning of relationships and values in the light of new information and knowledge (Giddens, 1991). Michael Schemmann has drawn attention to the ways in which Giddens and Beck see the contemporary shift towards continuing lifelong learning as a core element in what Giddens calls "institutionalised reflexivity", and as itself a vital part of the process of questioning and reshaping relationships (Schemmann, 2002; see also Field, 2000, pp 59-63).

We seem to have come a long way from the world of workers' education or the temperance movement. Yet, such 'postmodern conditions' may also explain the rising academic and wider interest in social capital. "Social capital", it has been suggested, "perhaps matches the spirit of an uncertain, questing age" (Schuller et al, 2000, p 38). The very insecurity of our social connections in a period of what Kirchhöfer (2000, p 15) calls "the individualised social shaping of the individual" may just be what is drawing our attention to their value. The interplay between radical reflexivity and individualisation tendencies has played its part in eroding fixed identities that are rooted in specific, given social milieux. Yet, precisely this shift towards a more fluid, open and contingent pattern of relations may have helped raise the prominence of the way in which our connections help to serve as a resource. It is this feature of relationships that is central to the concept of social capital.

Theories of social capital

Theories of social capital centre on the proposition that people's social networks are a valuable asset (Field, 2003a). At the micro level, most people know that personal relationships matter, and can be used to overcome shortcomings in other assets, a view illustrated in the popular British saying, "It isn't what you know, it's who you know". At a much more general level of analysis, people's connections provide a basis for wider social cohesion and stability. Complex societies hold together at least in part because people's everyday interactions with others enable them more generally to relate to and cooperate with one another – including strangers, and not just those whom they know directly – for mutual advantage. This is essentially Durkheim's view of the role of connections in a complex and modern society. They provide settings in which people learn the skills and qualities, such as trust, that are needed to get along and get things done in a reasonably predictable and certain manner, rather than simply existing as a "jumble of juxtaposed atoms" (Durkheim, 1933, p 226). Even in a period when social ties have loosened, and people are less tightly bound to their closest kin and neighbours than when Durkheim was writing, it remains the case that social solidarity in general depends on particular sets of relationships that tie individuals to one another, and facilitate reciprocity.

More recently, though, the idea of describing social ties as a form of capital has pointed to a further dimension of social connections. The contemporary debate has particularly focused on the idea of social capital as a resource, which people can then use in order to cooperate with others to pursue their own or shared goals. In this view, one factor that determines people's ability to achieve their goals is the nature and number of their social connections, and the extent to which these ties are reinforced by the existence of shared beliefs and values. This view of social capital has become increasingly influential in the social sciences, not least because there is an accumulating body of evidence to confirm the significance of people's connections for their well-being (in terms of wealth, health, education, relative immunity from crime, and so on), as well as for the democratic life of their wider society (this evidence is summarised in Field 2003a, ch 2).

Virtually all discussions of the theory of social capital start with the contributions of Pierre Bourdieu, James Coleman and Robert Putnam. Bourdieu and Coleman are probably the more original thinkers, and they are certainly responsible for much of the initial impetus behind today's debate. Bourdieu's approach, although slightly sketchy, has particularly influenced the way in which the concept is operationalised in this book. Above all, Bourdieu's usage is designed to address the way in which social capital is part of a wider set of structural relations and subjective beliefs that are bound up with inequalities of resources, and hence with inequalities of power. Yet, Bourdieu's conception is also incomplete, and I have adopted here a somewhat eclectic approach that draws selectively on other approaches to social capital, including those developed by Putnam and Coleman. Despite differences and controversies, though, there is broad agreement among those who use the concept that the core elements of social capital consist of personal connections and interpersonal interaction, together with the shared sets of values that are associated with these contacts.

Bourdieu's treatment of social capital emerged from his general attempt to develop a cultural anthropology of social reproduction. During the 1960s, Bourdieu became interested in the ways that members of the middle and upper strata were able to call on material and non-material resources to advance and secure their own interests, both in respect of those in lower social positions, but also in respect of other sub-groups in their own class position. It was precisely this context that gave rise to his widely debated concept of cultural capital, which denoted the ways in which middle- and upper-class people use cultural symbols as marks of social distinction, signalling and constituting their position in the class structure. The ability to enjoy Bach or jazz, for example, was not a sign of intrinsic superiority but a signal deployed by a particular social group in order to maintain superiority over other groups; Bach indicated the high culture of the haute bourgeoisie, jazz (and a taste for foreign cinema) a certain bohemianism among the more peripheral professional class. This set of signals, in the form of acquired taste, was then passed on to children. Moreover, according to Bourdieu, people's command of cultural capital did not just mirror their resources of financial capital. Shaped by family and school, cultural capital could to some extent operate independently of monetary holdings, and even compensate for lack of money as part of an individual's or a group's strategy to pursue power and status (Jenkins, 1992; Robbins, 2000).

Bourdieu's conception of social capital similarly emphasises the resources that people use to secure their own positional advantage. In a discussion first published in 1973 of the ways in which members of professional groups advance their interests (and those of their children), Bourdieu initially defined social capital as a "capital of social relationships which will provide, if necessary, useful 'supports': a capital of honourability and respectability which is often indispensable if one desires to attract clients in socially important positions, and which may serve as currency, for instance in a political career" (Bourdieu, 1977, p 503).

He subsequently provided the following general definition: "Social capital is the sum of resources, actual or virtual, that accrue to an individual or a group by virtue of possessing a durable network of more or less institutionalized relationships of mutual acquaintance and recognition" (Bourdieu and Wacquant, 1992, p 119).

In keeping with his view of capital as the product of accumulated labour, Bourdieu emphasised that connections require labour. Membership of a network gives rise to profits, and therefore requires "investment strategies, individual or collective" aimed at transforming contingent relationships into "social relationships that are directly usable in the short or long term"; for these to be effective over the long term, they must involve "durable obligations subjectively felt" (Bourdieu, 1980, p 2; 1986, p 249), with the act of investment taking the form of an "unceasing effort of sociability" (Bourdieu, 1986, p 250).

Bourdieu's usage of the concept was, then, part of a wider analysis of the foundations of social order. In an interview broadcast on West German television, Bourdieu compared the 'social field' to a casino: we gamble not only with the black chips that represent our economic capital, but also with the blue chips of our cultural capital and the red chips of our social capital (Alheit, 1996). In the game of life, then, we deploy a range of resources – including our network assets – in order to secure our positions and advance our interests.

Bourdieu is particularly significant for a number of reasons. The first is that he has had a remarkable influence for over two decades on educational studies. A landmark paper on education as a form of social reproduction, originally published in French in 1970, was rapidly translated into English (Bourdieu, 1977). It subsequently became an influential and widely cited text in critical educational studies, where Bourdieu essentially appeared to bolster a more or less Marxist analysis of education and social inequality. If his adoption by neo-Marxists in the English-speaking world led to a neglect of his wider concern with culture and social position, it was at least compatible with Bourdieu's own explicitly political purposes in much of his scholarly writing (Schinkel, 2003). However, it also led to a relative neglect of other aspects of Bourdieu's thinking in its relation to education. Most significant for this study, until the late 1990s, hardly any attention was paid in the English-speaking world to his analysis of social capital. A telling example of this is the neglect of Bourdieu's contribution by the American sociologist, James Coleman, despite the fact that the two had engaged with one another on other topics, including general theoretical approaches (see Coleman, 1991). An early paper by Bourdieu on social capital long went untranslated (Bourdieu, 1980).

Yet, it should also be said that Bourdieu's own treatment of the concept was short on depth. As Derek Robbins has said, Bourdieu largely treated the concept as an adjunct to, or even at times a dimension of, cultural capital (Robbins, 2000, p 36). If not easily defined as a Marxist himself, he nevertheless engaged with ideas that were deeply influenced by Marxism. He believed that ultimately "economic capital is at the root of all other types of capital" (Bourdieu, 1986, p 252), and that the various types of capital determined "the major classes of conditions of existence" on the basis of "different distributions of their total capital among the different kinds of capital" (Bourdieu, 1986, p 114). One consequence of this approach is that his theory remains rather one-dimensional, only acknowledging the social capital of the privileged. By definition, in his account, the poor and working class are defined by their lack of capital, whether social or of some other kind. In this book, by contrast, social capital is taken to be a universal human property: we all have ties and use them, so what matters is their range and nature.

Nor did Bourdieu really operationalise the idea for research purposes. In his early 'provisional notes' on the concept, Bourdieu described the notion of social capital as the "sole means" of accounting for the "principle of the social assets" that they may mobilise through mutual membership of a group; as examples, he listed family, old pupils of elite schools, membership of a select club and nobility (Bourdieu, 1980, p 2). In his monumental study of taste and distinction among the French bourgeoisie, which draws on a vast battery of empirical indicators of cultural capital, he furnished only one indicator of social capital: membership of golf clubs, which he thought was helpful in greasing the wheels of business life (Bourdieu, 1984, p 291). Subsequently, he attempted to operationalise the concept in further work on social reproduction, particularly in his critique of what he portrayed as the conformity and mediocrity of the French university system, where he examined the ways in which prominent scholars made use of their networks to advance the standing and prestige of their own disciplinary tribe, and to hinder the progress of others (Bourdieu, 1988). While there appears to be no particular difficulty in principle in using Bourdieu's concept as the basis for empirical research, this certainly remained a relatively undeveloped area in his own work.

Bourdieu also offers a slightly old-fashioned and individualistic treatment of social capital. As in so many other areas, his fieldwork came largely from his voluminous studies of the French haute bourgeoisie during the 1960s and early 1970s. His view of the family as subservient to the father smacks of its time and place, as does the supposed cachet arising from an appreciation of Bach, or the rebellious spirit signalled by a fondness for Miles Davis. Given his own intense commitment to political activism, there is remarkably little space for reflexivity, resistance and subversion (Boyne, 2002, p 117). It is taken for granted that a taste for Bach is generally accepted as signifying social superiority – hardly an idea that is likely to carry weight in the musical epoch of Britney and Eminem. There is little space for collective actors; individuals cultivate connections in order to maintain their superiority, and associational life is therefore simply an instrumental means to an end.

Yet, it is certainly possible to see a Bourdieuvian approach to social capital as interconnected with structural inequalities, and at the same time to treat it as a property of groups, and even as quintessentially a product of collective interaction. Also, we will not get far with the concept unless we accept that people's connections are rarely only, or even primarily, instrumental. While some may join a golf club or the Rotary as a way of furthering their business interests, most people tend to cooperate most effectively with people whom they like, and whose company they enjoy. The affective dimension of social capital has been greatly neglected in the literature, and Bourdieu is no exception.

Bourdieu's theory is not, then, without its flaws. Yet his emphasis on the importance of social capital as a source of power, and as a means for people to advance their interests and secure their relative advantage over the longer term, is a vital contribution to the debate. His stress on the work required to maintain social capital is also potentially significant, not least because it draws attention to the social and communicative skills involved in the processes of mutual cognition and recognition. Much about Bourdieu's conception appeals then, but, in order to place it in a wider intellectual context, it needs to be set alongside the other influential contributions of James Coleman and Robert Putnam.

Coleman has had a very different academic reception from Bourdieu. Whereas Bourdieu has suffered in the English-speaking world from the highly selective, partisan and uncritical embrace of critical educational researchers, Coleman has found a stronger reception in the mainstream of educational studies. His reputation stems from a series of investigations of educational attainment in American ghettos, in which Coleman was able to show that social capital could convey real benefits to otherwise poor and marginalised communities. Social capital, according to Coleman, represents a resource because it involves the expectation of reciprocity, and goes beyond any given individual to involve wider networks whose relationships are governed by a high degree of trust and shared values. Like Bourdieu, Coleman's concept of social capital was formulated as part of a wider attempt at explaining social order (Coleman, 1994).

In his attempt to construct a systematic theory of social order, Coleman drew on both economics and sociology. Coleman was influenced by the work of Gary Becker on human capital, which applied the principles of economics to the study of education, the family, health and discrimination, and did so within the framework of rational choice theory (Becker, 1964). Rational choice (or rational action) theory has been extremely influential in economics, and may therefore require little explanation. Its core belief is that all behaviour results from individuals pursuing their own interests in a rational manner; all social interaction is therefore a form of exchange. Coleman took from rational choice theory a view of society as an aggregation of individual behaviour. In explaining social order, then, Coleman proposed that system-level behaviour must be understood as the sum of individuals' preferences and actions.

Rational choice sociology assumes a highly individualistic model of human behaviour, with each person acting in ways that serve their own interests, regardless of the fate of others. It therefore has a considerable challenge in explaining why people cooperate with one another. Cooperation is rarely in the individual's interest, except in those rare circumstances where they are constrained into altruism – as in the care of their own children – or where there is a constraint upon the other agent to reciprocate. For Coleman, the attraction of social capital as a concept was that it offered a means of explaining how people nonetheless manage to cooperate with one another, across a wide range of situations.

From the outset, Coleman's interest in social capital was connected with the issue of children's educational attainment. An early study of peer group pressures among American adolescents was followed by a major survey of educational achievement and opportunity among six ethnic groups (Coleman et al, 1966). Subsequently, Coleman led a series of empirical studies comparing pupil achievement in private schools and public schools, showing that pupils tended to perform better at Catholic schools and schools with other religious affiliations even when other factors such as social class and ethnicity were taken into account (Coleman et al, 1982; Coleman and Hoffer, 1987). Coleman argued that the most important factor in explaining this pattern was the impact of community norms upon parents and pupils, which helped to endorse teachers' expectations. He concluded that communities were therefore a source of social capital that could offset some of the impact of social and economic disadvantage.

Coleman elaborated this analysis in a widely cited paper that explored the mutually beneficial relationship between social capital and human capital (Coleman, 1988-89). His central argument was that social capital made a positive contribution to the development of human capital. In this paper, he defined social capital as a useful resource available to an actor through his or her social relationships. It comprises a "variety of entities" that, Coleman surmised, "all consist of some aspect of social structures, and they facilitate certain actions of actors – whether persons or corporate actors – within the structure" (Coleman, 1988-89, p 98). Unlike human and physical capital, which are normally a private good whose ownership and returns reside with individuals, Coleman portrayed social capital quintessentially as a public good that is created by and may benefit not just those whose efforts are required to realise it, but all who are part of a structure (Coleman, 1988-89, p 116). It therefore demands cooperation between individuals who are nevertheless still pursuing their own individual interests.

In his late and most complete exploration of this theme, Coleman defined social capital as:

> ... the set of resources that inhere in family relations and in community social organisation and that are useful for the cognitive or social development of a child or young person. These resources differ for different persons and can constitute an important advantage for children and adolescents in the development of their human capital. (Coleman, 1994, p 300)

Elsewhere, he had defined social capital in respect of children's development as: "the norms, the social networks, and the relationships between adults and children that are of value for the child's growing up. Social capital exists within the family, but also outside the family, in the community" (Coleman, 1990, p 334).

Social capital is of value, then, not only in helping young people pass tests and gain credentials, but also in cognitive development and the evolution of a secure self-identity.

Coleman also believed that he could explain how social capital achieves such highly desirable outcomes. In his essay on social and human capital, relationships are held to establish obligations and expectations between people, building a general environment of trustworthiness, opening channels for information, and setting norms that endorse particular forms of behaviour while imposing sanctions on would-be free riders (Coleman, 1988-89, pp 102-4). In an argument that echoes some of the preoccupations of the communitarians, Coleman argued that the creation of social capital is assisted by "closure" between different networks, by stability, and by a common, shared ideology (Coleman, 1994, pp 104-8, 318-20). Coleman regarded closure – that is, the existence of multiple, dense, mutually reinforcing relations between different actors and institutions – as essential in providing not only for the repayment of obligations, but also for the imposition of sanctions. To take one example, it meant that clergy, neighbours and one's wider kin actively support teachers and parents in dissuading young people from playing truant or skipping their homework, and chivvying them to achieve in school. Social capital outside the family, simply stated, "exists in the interest, even the intrusiveness, of one adult in the activities of someone else's child" (Coleman, 1990, p 334).

Coleman shared with Bourdieu a belief in the patriarchal family as the archetypal cradle of social capital. In his broader theoretical framework, Coleman privileged the patriarchal family as the highest form of what he called "primordial" social organisation, which was distinguished by the fact that its origins lay "in the relationships established by childbirth". This was contrasted by Coleman with "constructed" forms of social organisation, which might come together for limited purposes, and represented weaker agencies of social control than primordial forms like the family (Coleman, 1991, pp 1-3). The only type of constructed organisation that he referred to in generally positive terms was organised religion (Coleman, 1990, p 336). So, for Coleman, the decline of the patriarchal family, and the growing responsibility of constructed organisations like schools and social services for socialising children were leading to a long-term erosion of the "social capital on which societal functioning has depended" (Coleman, 1991, p 9).

Coleman, then, took a frankly conservative view of church and family. In most European countries, and in not a few other societies, neither institution retains its unchallenged place in underpinning contemporary social life. More fundamentally, Coleman overplayed the role of close or dense ties, and underplayed that of weak or loose ties (Portes, 1998, p 5). Also, rather ironically for someone keen on rational choice theory, Coleman is remarkably negative about individualism. There are also some apparent inconsistencies in his analysis. For example, it could be argued that his account of social capital's role in building human capital leads logically to the view that rational individual choice provides a decidedly shaky basis for determining the distribution of skills. There are, then, serious weaknesses in his account. For the purposes of this study, Coleman's main strengths are his recognition that social capital could be an asset for disadvantaged social groups and not solely an instrument of privilege; and his interest in the mechanics of social networks.

The last of the trio of influential theorists is Robert Putnam. Putnam's preoccupations have been shaped more by debates within political science than sociology or economics. His study of social capital and governance in Italy used the concept of social capital to shed light on differences between the relatively affluent and civic-minded North and the relatively poor and ill-governed South. Putnam's definition, like Coleman's, stressed the role of social capital in supporting cooperation: "Social capital here refers to features of social organisation, such as trust, norms and networks, that can improve the efficiency of society by facilitating coordinated actions" (Putnam, 1993, p 167).

For Putnam, it contributes to collective action by increasing the potential costs to defectors; fostering robust norms of reciprocity; facilitating flows of information, including information on actors' reputations; embodying the successes of past attempts at collaboration; and setting the pattern for future cooperation (Putnam, 1993, p 173).

Since the mid-1990s, Putnam's work has hit the headlines in a way that is rare among political scientists. In a number of short papers and a hard-hitting book, he has drawn attention to what he sees as a potentially calamitous long-term decline in American stocks of social capital. Where much communitarian literature is extremely selective in its approach to evidence, Putnam offers a data-rich empirically-founded account of decline since the 1960s, and the cumulative impact of his evidence is highly persuasive (Putnam, 2000). On Putnam's data, political participation, associational membership, religious participation, volunteering, charity, work-based socialising and informal social networks have all shrunk dramatically since the 1960s. He relates this decline to survey findings showing that Americans' perceptions of honesty and trustworthiness have dropped from a peak in the mid-1960s. Although Putnam accepts that there are also countertrends, such as the growth of small self-help groups and youth volunteering, and the rise of new ways of communicating through the Internet and other technologies, he concludes that such evidence of revival and change certainly does not "outweigh the many other ways in which most Americans are less connected to our communities than we were two or three decades ago" (Putnam, 2000, p 180). This, he claims, is due principally to the rise of home-based electronic entertainments, above all television; and the slow replacement of an "unusually civic generation", forced into cooperative habits and values by "the great mid-century global cataclysm" of war and reconstruction by their egotistic children and grandchildren (Putnam, 2000, p 275).

Putnam's work has been enormously controversial (Field, 2003a, pp 37-9). In particular, his image of freefall in the stocks of social capital has been challenged for the US, and for many European nations as well. His indicators of civic engagement are selective. Where Coleman and Bourdieu focus on somewhat dated institutions and relatively close forms of bonding social capital, Putnam views the world of 19th- and 20th-century voluntary associations through rose-tinted glasses. A number of political scientists have noted his neglect of political decisions in creating – or damaging – opportunity structures that enable civic participation (Maloney et al, 2000a, 2000b; Braun, 2002, p 10). Putnam also tends to portray social capital as a remarkably positive, unproblematic public good. Bourdieu's interest in its contribution to social inequality and cronyism is completely alien to Putnam's vision of the good community. So, if Putnam's highly influential account seems to be even more problematic than those of Coleman and Bourdieu, a doubter might well wonder whether we should simply abandon the concept altogether.

Nor is this to exhaust the concept's weaknesses, at least as developed so far. One inescapable feature of all three foundational writers is the 'gender-blindness' of their work. Putnam pays limited and somewhat unsatisfying attention to the gendering of social capital (Putnam, 2000, pp 94-5), while both Coleman and Bourdieu largely ignore the issue (Morrow, 1999). Yet, much civic engagement is highly gendered (Lowndes, 2004), and Coleman's inherently conservative view of the family is not merely dated but has significant consequences for his analytical framework (Blaxter and Hughes, 2001). The obvious question arising from this general reluctance to explore the gender dimension of a clearly gendered practice is whether the concept itself is fundamentally flawed, or whether this is simply a product of a rather traditional approach to the evidence. Given the significance of gender relations to learning in adult life, they cannot be neglected in this study. However, I can see no intrinsic reason why attention to gender cannot be combined with the study of people's networks, and the access to resources that these networks can bring.

What, then, does the idea of social capital bring to the analysis of relationships and behaviour? If the concept does add to our toolkit for social analysis, its chief contribution surely lies in its focus on networks and relationships as a resource. In this book, I follow Coleman and Putnam in viewing social capital as a distributed resource, which is not the exclusive property of the privileged elite, but is also created and mobilised by subordinate and intermediary groups of all kinds. Yet, if Bourdieu failed to recognise the importance of social capital resources to disadvantaged groups, Putnam and Coleman gloss over the role of inequalities (Hibbitt et al, 2001, p 145). They also tend to assume that social capital is a Good Thing, and that more is almost invariably better. In my own emphasis on the dark side of social capital – on its 'negative externalities' – I am drawing explicitly on Bourdieu's notion of capital as a positional asset that people can use in order to pursue their own advantage and consolidate their own position relative to others, and not simply as invariably forming a communal good.

This helps to lead us towards a more differentiated version of social capital, which recognised that it comes in different forms, each of which may have distinctive consequences. In his work on social capital in the development process, Michael Woolcock has tried to identify three broad categories of social connections:

1. binding social capital, comprised of ties between like people in similar situations, such as immediate family, close friends and neighbours;
2. bridging social capital, which is made up of more distant ties with like persons, such as loose friendships and workmates; and
3. linking – or scaling – social capital, which reaches out to unlike people in dissimilar situations, such as those who are entirely outside the community, thus enabling members to leverage a far wider range of resources than are available within the community (Woolcock, 1998), pp 13-14).

The analysis in this volume broadly adopts Woolcock's differentiated approach, rather than trying to treat social capital resources as comprised of relatively homogeneous sets of connections and norms. The next section of this chapter examines the relevance of this discussion to the field of lifelong learning.

The importance of social capital to lifelong learning

How can the concept of social capital help us to understand lifelong learning? Little direct help can be found in the writings of the foundational authors whose work was summarised earlier. While all three have written about education in the context of social capital, their interest was largely confined to schools or university education. Recent research in the London-based Wider Benefits of Learning Research Centre has started to explore the relationships to some extent, but largely in terms of the impact of adult learning on the creation of social capital rather than the other way round (Schuller et al, 2004). Relatively little work has so far been conducted into the influence of social capital on lifelong learning.

At the most general level, the association between social capital and lifelong learning can be viewed as a process of dynamic mutual inter-cognition. Putnam and Bourdieu both recognised this quite explicitly, at least in general terms. Putnam has done so in his depiction of civic engagement as an intrinsically educational process. He views associations as the schools of democracy, where people are taught the two-times-table of civic behaviour, and develop capacities for reciprocity and trust, which then spill over the borders of their own group, and shape their attitudes and behaviour in the public sphere more generally. Bourdieu equally views the connections of the privileged as sites where people learn reciprocity and trust, and also learn how to recognise the limits beyond which trust and reciprocity are not extended. Outside the valued networks and associations of the privileged, social capital creates institutionalised mistrust. However, this too is a learning process – a process, as Bourdieu puts it, of constant mutual cognition and (re)cognition. At the most general level, then, the creation and recreation of social capital can be seen as in itself a process of continuing (re)cognition.

More specifically, it is clear that people acquire very particular skills through their connections. Such skills are derived from the practices of cooperation, whether in formalised associations or through more loose connections. As well as the capacity for trust, which has been widely debated in the literature, these include such capacities and qualities as communications, organisational skills, tolerance towards others, confidence and a sense of self-worth, and enterprise (or a willingness to seize the initiative). Furthermore, in contrast to much institutionalised education, which is aimed largely at young people of particular age groups, learning in and through social connections may to some extent increase with age: "The role of social networks and norms in fostering a culture of learning is important throughout the entire lifecycle" (CEC, 2003, p 24).

There is also the prospect of a more indirect relationship, in that civic engagement may endow an individual with affective capacities that increase the prospect of seeking personal transformation through education. One British study of adult students on access courses found that two thirds had previously been active in voluntary organisations; the author concluded that "active participation … increases an individual's perception of power and self-worth", and reduced levels of aversion among adults towards the risks associated with a return to schooling (Benn, 1996, p 173). Such emotional, moral and (auto)biographical competences appear to be resources of growing significance in late modernity, with its constant demands for identity renewal (Alheit, 1994).

Finally, social capital can contribute to learning by creating pressures from peers and other well-regarded individuals, such as parents. James Coleman's argument, stripped to its essentials, is that closely knit communities with strongly shared norms can form a powerful consensus around the value of skills, knowledge and qualifications, as well as posing persuasive negative sanctions on those who are seen to deviate from this consensus. It is worth noting that Coleman does not see the community and its norms as having any direct connection with learning in itself, but rather concentrates on social capital as a form of social control that favours those who are committed to the approved institutions of schooling. Perhaps this is one reason why his interest in human capital is confined primarily to school attendance and attainment. However, it is equally conceivable that adults' learning aspirations are affected by their connections, and by the norms of those with whom they connect. Quite obviously, the influence of social capital can be negative, at least potentially, where the connections and their norms are such as to create and maintain a low aspiration culture, rather than fostering one that aims high.

Social capital, then, can promote learning. Yet learning is not solely a simple by-product of social connections. People also bring their existing skills and knowledge to their connections. Again, this may well be at the general level of people's dispositions, such as the propensity to trust other people and to enjoy their company. Or it may be more specific, and at the level of particular cognitive, interpersonal or affective skills. All other things being equal, it is likely that people who have these skills and knowledge will be more likely to feel comfortable in voluntary associations and public life more generally than those who do not; and they will also be much more likely to take leading positions than those who have few such skills or knowledge. As shown earlier in this chapter, it is very well known that those who participate in voluntary associations tend to have better educational qualifications than non-participants, and they are more likely to have left the educational system after the minimum legal leaving age. According to survey data for the Irish Republic, the highly qualified also show significantly higher levels of interpersonal trust than those with the lowest levels, and they are more likely to believe that collective action can influence public decisions (NESF, 2003, pp 53, 60). The same survey also suggests that people's network types are also associated with education: the highly educated are most likely to rely on work associates for social support, and the least educated are far more likely to rely on family and neighbours (NESF, 2003, p 59). As ever, it is hard to disentangle cause and effect, but the nature of the relationship seems fairly clear.

If indeed it is true that people gain tangible benefits from having more connections and gaining access to wider fields of civic activity, then it appears that people's social capital resources may partly be determined by their educational level. This may not only be a matter of education helping people to acquire and strengthen their capital of connections, but also of enabling them to turn social capital into an applicable resource. Yet, even this should be seen as an iterative course of action, where the mobilisation of social capital resources remains a process that intrinsically involves cognition and (re)cognition. It is thus to be seen as an active and interactive process in which new meanings and understandings are constantly being reproduced and (re)created at the same time.

Thus far, the picture drawn is highly consistent with Coleman's diagnosis of the mutually beneficial interplay of social capital with human capital (Coleman, 1988-89). Even though Coleman was writing about the acquisition of educational credentials by young people in schools, my argument up to this point suggests that the same relationship is likely to hold good for learning in adult life as well. To extend Coleman's account in this way is to suggest that people in strong communities are more likely to take part in learning, because they will share attitudes that favour learning, and will therefore encourage one another to engage willingly with the education and training system. Nor do we have to accept Coleman's relatively narrow definition of social capital to accept that social capital may be expected to promote learning. People with the largest and most tested networks can be expected to have more access to information, including information both about the potential value of new skills or knowledge (for example, the potential of information technology to solve a practical problem), as well as about the potential effectiveness of different types of learning resource (for example, the quality of an adult education provider).

This simple hypothesis appears to be supported by at least some empirical evidence. The large-scale study by Elsdon and his associates has demonstrated in depth the variety of opportunities that small-scale voluntary and community-based organisations create for informal and incidental learning, as well as increasing the demand for more formal training and organisational development (Elsdon et al, 1995). We might reasonably expect, then, that people with the best connections are more likely to take part in lifelong learning.

However, this is to make a number of assumptions that may not be justified, such as the idea that strongly shared values will automatically be favourable towards adult learning. It is at least conceivable that strong communities may share a negative view of adult learning. Moreover, I have already argued that Coleman used a somewhat undifferentiated definition of social capital, which overemphasised rather close types of tie such as family and church. Also, if we accept that we need a differentiated view of social capital, then it follows that the different types of social capital may function in different ways. Furthermore, we need to distinguish between the differing capabilities that are endowed by learning and network resources. The interplay of social capital and lifelong learning always involves relations of power, a factor largely neglected by those who follow Coleman and Putnam; but, whereas Bourdieu generally treats power and authority as vested only in elite groups, who use their power *over* others, my own perspective is a more polycentric and relational one. The approach taken here is that people who are relatively disadvantaged in their access to financial or human capital can still turn to their network resources and deploy them actively in promoting and advancing their interests. Finally, network resources do not always or even constitute *power over*, but also and perhaps more frequently represent a *power to* – they constitute a capability that is in itself empowering, and network assets can also unleash other capabilities (Sen, 1999). They are therefore potentially a force for human freedom.

If there are different types of social capital, it seems likely that some types may be especially linked to particular forms of learning. Through the creation and internalisation of achievement norms, bonding social capital is likely to favour participation in formal education and training. However, where bonding capital is more closely associated with norms of low achievement, it is likely to discourage participation in formal education and training. As for informal learning, close bonding ties may well generate those affective and social competences that are best suited to routine and habitual forms of interaction, as well as facilitating the sharing of those types of information that are not easily passed on among mere acquaintances, for whatever reason. Close ties, then, may well favour informal learning within the immediate group, but they also limit access to skills and information that are not readily available within the group.

Bridging and linking social capital may well be associated with formal education and training, but may also offer alternative – and arguably more reliable – ways of gaining access to new ideas, information and skills. It has been suggested that looser ties may help foster reflexive learning, as well as promoting the acquisition and development of reflexive practices themselves, since "flexibly structured networks ... allow actors to perform and position themselves in exchangeable roles and settings" (Edwards et al, 2002, p 534). Linking social capital is, in general, more likely to be associated with exposure to a multiplicity of information and knowledge. It might be expected that, other things being equal, exposure to heterogeneous information through a variety of loose ties is likely to promote ambition and effort, as well as fostering ingenuity and creativity. Similarly, it seems probable that looser networks will promote those affective and social competences that are best suited to coping with change and disruption, forming part of what has been called a kind of 'risk insurance' (Kade and Seitter, 1998, p 54).

At this stage, a speculative typology may be helpful, at least for heuristic purposes. Figure 1.1 offers some tentative assessments of the potential influence of social capital on lifelong learning. Of course, these speculations may seem neat and logical but, in practice, all social behaviour is path dependent, so that historical context and structural factors such as social position and perhaps gender will also shape patterns of learning in ways that may reinforce or undermine the influence of social capital. Also, of course, people engage actively with structures, with social capital constituting one of many resources at their disposal.

Bonding, bridging and linking ties may all contribute to learning, then, but they seem likely to do so in different and rather contrasting ways. However, deciding which is the most effective is not easy. Each has its strengths, and each its weaknesses: as Morgan puts it, strong "achievement norms stifle ingenuity/creativity and heterogeneous information breaks down discipline" (Morgan, 2000, p 593). As in other areas of social life, each type of social capital will be good for different purposes. If we follow Bourdieu's approach, and view social capital as one of a number of distinct but interrelated capitals, it follows that the interplay between learning and networks must at the same time involve relations of power. The following chapters offer some empirical evidence on aspects of the relationship, drawn from qualitative and quantitative studies of social capital and adult learning in Northern Ireland. This should help us to put some firm flesh onto the rather skeletal framework that has been elaborated here.

Figure 1.1: Bonding, bridging and linking social capital, and their possible effects on lifelong learning

Type of social capital	Possible effects on lifelong learning
Bonding – dense but bounded networks, homogeneity of membership, high levels of reciprocity and trust, exclusion of outsiders	Free exchange of ideas, information and skills within group; strong influence on identity formation among children; high trust placed in information received, limited access to new and varied knowledge from outside group, and low trust of knowledge from outside group; relationship to education system likely to be highly traditionalist in orientation
Bridging – loose and open-ended networks, heterogeneity of membership, shared norms and common goals, levels of trust and reciprocity may be more limited	Relatively free exchange of a variety of ideas, information, skills and knowledge within group and between own and other groups; potential resources for identity maintenance and renewal among adults; high trust in information and knowledge from within group (and possibly from others with shared values); relationship with formal education system highly context-dependent
Linking – loose and open-ended networks, variety of membership, shared norms and common goals, levels of trust and reciprocity may be circumscribed by competing demands	Relatively free exchange of a variety of ideas, information, skills and knowledge within group and between own and other groups; some trust in information and knowledge from within group (and possibly from others with shared values); open resources to support identity change among adults; relationship with formal education system highly conditional

TWO

Networks, schooling and learning in adult life: interview evidence

Despite a long tradition of debate over adult education and citizenship, research into the influence of social capital on lifelong learning is still a relative newcomer. This is not simply a matter of changing terminology, though the emerging influence of the concepts of lifelong learning and social capital since the 1990s has certainly played an important role in breathing new life into a well-established line of inquiry. It is also true that the mainstream debate over adult education and active citizenship has been highly normative. For many of the participants, the collection and analysis of empirical evidence took second place to the critique of policy and development of practice. Although some researchers noted the empirical association between participation in learning and involvement in the wider society, the dominant voices in the debate were much more concerned with the restatement of adult education's social and political purpose, a concern that was often accompanied by anguished analyses of the decline of workers' education and political education.

Such passions and anxieties may now appear somewhat arcane. Yet an interest in the wider social contexts of lifelong learning is surely not confined to the ranks of aging adult educators like myself. Nor, despite my classical training in social and economic research methods, can I bring myself to eject values and social purpose from the analysis of education and training. My own work has long been marked by an interest in which adults get to participate in learning, and of what kinds; and which adults get to be marginalised and excluded. My initial interest in social capital was partly inspired by a concern to explain patterns of participation in adult learning in Northern Ireland, and partly by a continuing curiosity over the historical and contemporary relations between adult education and active citizenship.

In an early paper on the connections between social capital and lifelong learning, Tom Schuller and I argued that the concept not only offered a potential counterbalance to what we saw as the overemphasis on human capital in the dominant literature (Schuller and Field, 1998). We also suggested ways in which the idea of social capital might help pinpoint some of those social relationships and practices that appeared to promote participation in adult learning (Schuller and Field, 1998). Subsequently, an analysis of the International Adult Literacy Survey results for 17 western nations showed that countries that scored high in respect of adult education participation also tended to score highly on participation in voluntary associations, and generally showed higher levels of trust in other people (Tuijnman and Boudard, 2001, p 40). A broadly similar pattern emerges when using rather different data, drawn from the European Values Survey and the European Labour Force Survey (Figure 2.1). Family connections have also been shown to have a very powerful influence on people's participation in learning, with an impact that apparently stretches back for at least three generations (Gorard and Rees, 2002). These findings seem to confirm the initial hunch of our 1998 paper, which argued that people's connections are somehow tied to their learning, in ways that could have considerable practical significance.

This chapter takes the analysis further, drawing on the findings of a field-based study of adult learning and social capital in Northern Ireland. The study was provoked in part by the observation of a somewhat distinctive pattern of educational attainment in Northern Ireland. It is the conventional wisdom of adult education scholarship, buttressed by much empirical evidence, that those people and social groups who have the highest school qualifications tend also to maintain their educational advantage throughout their adult lives, by continuing to participate in organised learning (Cross, 1981; McGivney, 1991; Sargant, 1997). Northern

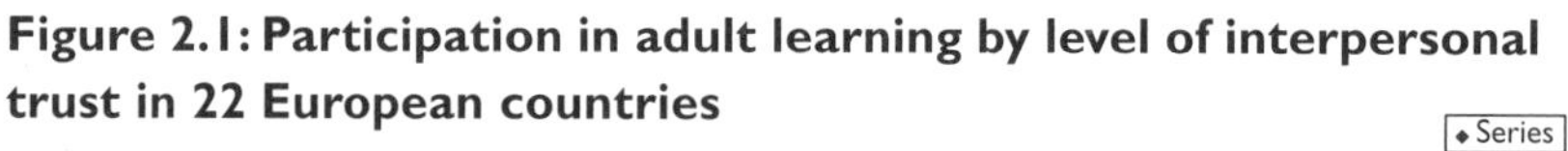

Figure 2.1: Participation in adult learning by level of interpersonal trust in 22 European countries

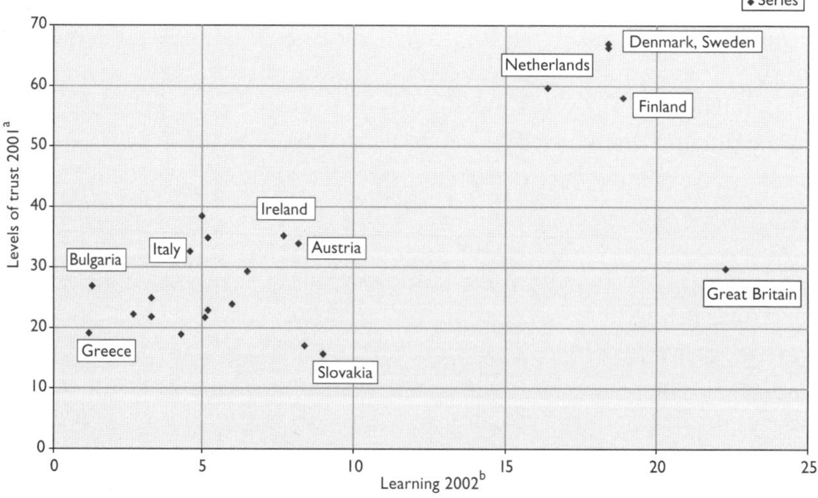

Notes: [a] percentage agreeing with the statement: 'most people can be treated'; taken from Halman, 2001, p 44); [b] Percentage of adult population (aged 25-64) participating in education and training in 2002; taken from CEC (2004, p 83).

Sources: European Labour Force Survey; World Values Survey

Ireland, however, diverges from this standard picture of lifelong 'human capital accumulation'. Although its schools system achieves some of the highest examinations results to be found in the UK, its adult population also shows the lowest rate of participation in organised learning. As there is also compelling evidence that the overall level of social capital in Northern Ireland is comparatively high, the research sought to establish whether this was in any way connected with what appeared to be a somewhat unusual pattern of educational achievement. This chapter presents an analysis of interview data gathered in the course of a research project funded through the Economic and Social Research Council's (ESRC) Learning Society Programme. First, though, a brief description of lifelong learning in Northern Ireland may be helpful in providing a background to the study.

Education and adult learning in Northern Ireland

As one of the UK's four federal components, Northern Ireland has its own highly distinctive education and training system. Since the later 1980s, the education system has undergone a period of considerable policy transformation, but to date its main defining features have remained largely unchanged since the passage of the 1947 Education Act. Secondary schooling is sharply divided into grammar and high schools, with a fiercely competitive transfer test at 11+. In addition, primary and secondary education is administratively divided between so-called 'voluntary schools', which are managed by the main churches but grant-aided by the government; and the 'controlled' schools, which are administered by local education boards; although there is a small number of grant-maintained integrated schools, this system means that the vast majority of pupils are educated in schools where virtually all of the pupils are either Catholics or Protestants. Third-level education is provided by the Institutes of Further and Higher Education, whose functions broadly mirror those of the further education system in Britain, and by the universities; other than in highly prescribed areas, such as teacher education, there is no formal segregation at this level.

Adult learners in Northern Ireland are provided for by a complex range of institutions that will be familiar to many British and Irish readers. As well as the Institutes of Further and Higher Education and the universities, and a broad range of work-based training providers, there is a vibrant Workers' Educational Association and a comparatively well-developed voluntary sector. As well as the usual sources of public funding, adult learning in Northern Ireland is treated by the European Commission as one of its least-advantaged regions, and therefore receives considerable support from the European Commission's Structural Funds. Finally, the Belfast-based Educational Guidance Service for Adults, which now covers the whole of Northern Ireland, is widely regarded in the UK and beyond as a beacon among adult information and guidance services.

Educational attainment in Northern Ireland is characterised by a marked divergence between initial and continuing education. In initial education – essentially, school through to university – overall performance is high. One way of measuring this is to look at the proportion who perform well in schools examinations (Table 2.1). So far as the GCSE is concerned, the percentage gaining the minimum normally required for consideration by higher education institutions is similar to Scotland's, and well above the rate in England or Wales. Similarly, Northern Ireland and Scotland are significantly ahead of the rest of the UK in the proportion of pupils gaining the minimum threshold for university entrance in their A Levels (or SCE Highers). Since the late 1980s, however, Northern Ireland has diverged from all the rest of the UK – including Scotland – in respect of the proportion who leave school with no qualifications whatever.

Academic attainment in Northern Ireland's school system is ahead of all the rest of the UK apart from Scotland. And the lead is even stronger when it comes to participation in higher education. Conventionally, participation rates are measured by the 'age participation index' (API), which is a ratio of the number of entrants to higher education divided by the total number in the population from the age group that supplies higher education students. The API has a number of flaws, and its tendency to support an inflated participation rate for Scotland is not among the most important. Tables 2.2 and 2.3 therefore offer slightly different evidence based on the API. Table 2.2 gives the API for the four UK nations as a

Table 2.1: Examinations achievements of pupils in schools in the UK (1993/94 and 2001/02) (%)

	Five or more grades A-C in GCSE or SCE Standard Grades	No graded results at GCSE	Two or more GCE A Levels/three or more SCE Highers
2001/02			
England	51.6	5.4	37.6
Scotland	60.4	4.6	39.4
Wales	50.5	7.6	30.6
Northern Ireland	58.7	4.4	43.4
1993/94			
England	43.3	7.7	19.2
Scotland	48.4	8.4	29.7
Wales	39.4	10.1	19.7
Northern Ireland	48.5	4.8	30.0

Sources: Church (1996); Causer and Virdee (2004)

Table 2.2: Participation rate in higher education by domicile for selected age groups (2001-02)

	England	Wales	Scotland	Northern Ireland	UK
17	0.4	0.7	14.1	0.3	1.6
18-20	27.5	29.0	27.6	33.0	27.76
21-24	13.0	14.5	12.8	18.5	13.2
25-29	4.9	6.1	5.7	5.1	5.0
30-39	3.5	4.3	4.1	3.1	3.6

Source: HESA (2003, p 25). The participation rate used here is a snapshot for each age group; it should not be confused with the initial entry rate, which is a measure of flow into higher education (HESA, p 8). The figures cover all higher education, whether taking place in a university or in other types of institution.

Table 2.3: Percentage of young entrants from social classes IIIM, IV or V into higher education institutions in the four UK nations

	1998	2000	2002
UK	25.1	25.4	28.4
England	24.9	25.3	27.9
Wales	26.4	25.9	29.8
Scotland	24.1	24.4	28.0
Northern Ireland	33.6	32.9	41.3

Source: Taken from the reports on performance indicators published by the higher education funding bodies, at www.hefce.ac.uk/learning/perfind

crude ratio of entrants to members of the relevant age group; by this measure, it looks as though Northern Ireland and Scotland both share a similar position, comparatively well above that for England and Wales. Table 2.3, by contrast, looks at the proportion of young higher education entrants from manual working-class families; for this group, the participation rate at higher education institutions in Northern Ireland is considerably higher than in any of the three nations of Britain. So in terms of its academic strengths, the Northern Ireland education system is proving remarkably successful for young people, particularly those from otherwise disadvantaged backgrounds.

Of course, the achievement of academic qualifications is only one measure of attainment. It could be the case that young people in Northern Ireland do well academically because they are working systematically towards success in specific qualifications, and not because they are well educated in a more general sense. These is some limited evidence for this hypothesis in the findings of the Programme for International Student Assessment (PISA), a collaborative study among 32 member states of the Organisation for Economic Co-operation and Development (OECD), conducted among 15-year-olds in 2000 in three broad areas of 'literacy': reading, mathematics and science. Because it used standardised assessment tools, it did not measure attainment against a specific national or local curriculum, but focused on problems that pupils might expect to encounter in adult life. Northern Ireland came slightly below England in respect of reading and mathematics, and somewhat further behind in respect of scientific literacy[1]. However, as in England, pupils in Northern Ireland scored significantly above the OECD average on all three sets of indicators, falling in each case comfortably into the top third of countries studied (Johnston, 2002). So PISA does not provide significant support for the belief that young people in Northern Ireland are merely trained to perform well in tests. By international standards, this is a society of educational high achievers.

PISA also provides evidence of a further distinguishing characteristic of the Northern Ireland system: the scale of the variation around the statistical mean. In each of the areas studied, pupils were categorised into five levels of proficiency. In all three domains, Northern Ireland showed a greater spread of achievement than either England or the Republic of Ireland, with more falling into the top classification and more in the bottom, and notably fewer in the groups in the middle. This bipolar distribution is shown below for the case of reading proficiency (Table 2.4), for example, but the distribution is little different in mathematics and science. While this is not likely to be the consequence of one single cause, it is highly unlikely that it is entirely unconnected with the existence of selection at 11+ in Northern Ireland, with the consequent division of the schools population into two.

On balance, though, the evidence points to relatively high levels of academic attainment as compared with the rest of the UK. Although there is a question mark over the extent to which this relative advantage is confined to performance in examinations rather than background understanding and knowledge, PISA suggests that Northern Ireland's initial education system is still well ahead of most OECD countries. Moreover, it should be remembered that this level of achievement takes place in a context of marked relative deprivation. If hardly poor by global standards, Northern Ireland remains a low-income society when judged by the norms of Western Europe. Average gross weekly incomes are around a

Table 2.4: Reading literacy: proportion at the highest and lowest proficiency levels, PISA 2000 (England, Scotland, Republic of Ireland and Northern Ireland) (%)

	At or below Level 1	Level 5
England	13	16
Scotland	12	15
Republic of Ireland	11	14
Northern Ireland	15	16
OECD average	18	10

Source: Johnston (2002, p 161); EYPU (2002)

quarter less than the UK average, and for much of the 1990s Northern Ireland had the highest claimant unemployed rate of any UK region, as well as far and away the highest proportion of long-term unemployed. These are not characteristics that are usually associated with strong academic performance. Rather, the more usual pattern is that it is the most well-to-do regions and nations that are best able to convert other resources into educational credentials. Yet by the standards of the UK, and by comparison with much richer countries in the OECD, Northern Ireland is characterised by very strong achievement at different stages of schooling. This then leads to one of the highest proportions of young people entering university of any UK region[2].

When it comes to education and training in adult life, though, the picture is reversed. From coming top of the UK league for schools performance, Northern Ireland sinks straight to the bottom. Table 2.5 shows that the proportion of people of working age who receive any job-related training is consistently lower in Northern Ireland than elsewhere in the UK. This might be explained partly by local economic structures, such as the dominance of small firms and family enterprises in Northern Ireland. Much harder to explain, given the level of attainment in schools, is the relatively high proportion of adults who have no qualifications. Table 2.6 shows that, although the trend in all four UK nations is downwards, the proportion with no formal qualifications in Northern

Table 2.5: Proportion of workforce receiving job-related training in the UK (1986-2001) (%)

	England	Scotland	Wales	Northern Ireland
Males				
2001	13.8	14.5	16.0	12.2
1995[a]	13.7	13.3	13.7	9.9
1991	15.0	13.7	13.3	11.1
1986	11.8	8.6	10.6	9.4
Females				
2001	17.6	15.9	20.7	15.2
1995	15.3	12.6	15.6	12.6
1991	15.5	12.4	14.0	13.0
1986	10.5	6.3	9.9	7.9

Note: [a] Due to changes in the Labour Force Survey in 1994, data from 1995 onwards are not comparable with earlier years.
Sources: Church (1996, p 71); Causer and Virdee (2004, p 66)

Table 2.6: Proportion of UK workforce with no formal qualifications (1995-2001) (%)

	England	Scotland	Wales	Northern Ireland
2001	14.6	14.7	17.1	23.7
1995	16.8	18.0	15.1	26.1

Source: Church (1996, p 84); Causer and Virdee (2004, p 65)

Table 2.7: Percentage of adult population participating in formal and informal learning (2003) (%)

England	Scotland	Wales	Northern Ireland
39	42	38	30

Source: Aldridge and Tuckett (2003)

Ireland has remained stubbornly around 10 percentage points above that in England. Finally, Table 2.7 demonstrates that take-up of general adult education is also much lower in Northern Ireland than it is elsewhere in the UK. Taken together, these figures produce a consistent picture of low participation in adult learning that contrasts starkly with the remarkable levels of schools attainment. This pattern requires some explanation, and the research project undertaken in the ESRC's Learning Society Programme was aimed to answer this question.

In addressing this question, one possible line of enquiry concerned the role of Northern Ireland's very distinctive social structures. It is impossible to spend time in Northern Ireland without being struck by the strength of family and churches as the twin poles of everyday life. Even a casual visitor will probably also notice the plethora of voluntary and community-based organisations that appear to thrive in every town and city, as well as in many of the smaller communities.

Such anecdotal evidence is confirmed by much more systematic studies of social networks, showing that overall levels of civic engagement are well above those found in Britain (Murtagh, 2002). Mary Daly's recent analysis of survey data goes into further detail, showing that if overall levels of social capital in Northern Ireland are relatively high, they are based on a pattern of relating to other people that is highly distinctive (Daly, 2004). Predictably, family turns out to be far more significant than in Britain; there is also a suggestion that matriarchal relations have particular importance, with some 23% of adults in Northern Ireland seeing their mother at least once a day, against only 9% in Britain (Daly, 2004, p 55). Family also took first place in providing social support in both Britain and Northern Ireland, though in both cases people tended to look mainly to their spouse for help in a crisis; what was notable was that people in Britain are markedly more likely to turn to their spouse/partner, and markedly less likely to turn to their mother; while close friends only feature significantly as a source of support when one felt low, they were more likely to be cited in Britain than in Northern Ireland (Daly, 2004, p 59). Finally, within an overall pattern of high participation in both societies, membership of church groups and charity organisations was markedly higher in Northern Ireland, while other forms of voluntary organisation tended to command higher levels of involvement in Britain (Daly 2004, p 62).

The overall picture is, then, one of a society that has kept its traditional sources of support intact, and shows a relatively high level of homogeneity. Given the popular preconceptions about social life in Northern Ireland, it may be worth adding that this pattern is shared broadly across the community, regardless of religion or social class (Daly, 2004, p 66; Murtagh, 2002). Yet this is counterbalanced by the corrosive effects of sectarian hostility and the perceived threats that may face people when they leave the security of family and neighbourhood. A recent study of undergraduate lifestyles illustrates this point: students in Northern Ireland are much more likely to feel unsafe, even in their accommodation, than are their counterparts in any other UK region (Table 2.8). Given that overall levels of reported violent crime are much the same in Northern Ireland as Scotland, it seems that people's sense of security is shaped to some extent by perceptions as well as the real risks, but what is clear is that in Northern Ireland even young people in a relatively protected environment feel less secure than do fellow students across the water. To walk among strangers feels risky. This, then, provides some basis for analysing patterns of participation in adult learning, which in Northern Ireland takes place against a background of high stocks of social capital overall, but distributed in quite distinctive ways.

Initial and continuing education: perspectives from focus groups

The ESRC study used a number of different approaches to the analysis of social capital and adult learning, but with an emphasis on qualitative methods (Field and Schuller, 2000). Most of the new data gathered for the study were collected through interviews; in particular, through 10 group interviews with people whose jobs brought them into contact with adult learners, such as personnel officers or recruiters, organised by economic sector; and 30 face-to-face interviews with people responsible

Table 2.8: Percentage of students feeling safe all of the time, Northern Ireland and Scotland

	Northern Ireland	Scotland
In your accommodation	60	80
Walking around university (daytime)	63	88
Walking around university (night-time)	27	40

Source: Sodexho (2004, p 36)

in some way for managing programmes of education and training. The interviews were held with people from across Northern Ireland (though a majority came from Greater Belfast), and with people from the voluntary and community sectors as well as from business, government and education.

One point worth making is that the focus groups were themselves a particularly good way of studying social capital. Northern Ireland is a comparatively small society, and we expected that some, possibly all, the participants would already know most of the other key players in their sector. In the event, we found that most participants already knew one another and greeted one another by name; anyone who did not already know other participants was quickly introduced. One consequence of this was that some participants already knew what to expect from their colleagues, particularly if they suspected that a familiar bee might be about to buzz in their bonnet. Another consequence was that the group interviewees were confident and articulate, and indeed gave every sign of enjoying a sociable exchange with fellow professionals on matters of common interest. This is not to claim that there was no interplay of power and conflict of interests in the focus groups, but rather that the conflicts and power relations were not solely those between researchers and researched. As can be seen in the transcripts, some people were more vocal than others, and occasionally some tried to silence other participants (mostly without success).

Most of the focus groups began with participants expressing views – sometimes quite strong views – on the very short introduction. Some of our interviewees challenged our picture of Northern Ireland's educational attainment. After 10 minutes of argument in the software industry meeting, for example, an experienced industrialist concluded:

Harry[3] I think what's come out of this, is you are surprising us with the excellence of our schools!

In the focus group for people working in rural development, participants also thought we were over-optimistic about the state of Northern Ireland's education. Having introduced the background to our study, the facilitator started with the following question, which provoked an immediate and very clear answer:

LS If we can just start off looking at the first question, the disparity, whether it exists within your particular sector.

Niall Yes! [*laughter*]

LS	Yes?
Niall	The answer is 'Yes'.
Kate	We've certainly looked at it at an area level rather than the regional level which you've looked at. Our figures are more alarming, with – in terms of adult figures we have 50% of people in our area with no formal qualifications, rather than I think it was 26% there, the Northern Ireland figure.

In fact, as already noted, the level of academic achievement in Northern Ireland's schools system has risen significantly since the 1970s. There was some awareness of this change, if often limited. In the words of a male Protestant professional, during the rural development focus group,

Niall	I just kind of wondered, is there any cause, is the difference a simple historical thing? Is it just the younger population that's boosting these figures in terms of A Levels and O Levels? And historically the sort of 35, 40+ age group didn't have that type of education and maybe that's what's skewing the figures. Is there any figures that look back at the fifties and sixties and see what sort of education did they achieve in school, as opposed to now?

More commonly, participants had a rather dated view of attainment in the schools system, but those who spoke clearly felt at ease in expressing disagreement or surprise at the facilitator's introductory remarks on the topic. So the first finding from the focus groups was that participants felt completely confident in challenging the summary picture that the researchers had painted of a high-attainment education system.

By contrast, there was less surprise over our description of adult learning. Only the software industry participants expressed a degree of doubt about the low level of participation in adult learning that we reported. One of its members speculated that this might be due to the particular nature of the industry:

Brian	But there are in our business, in our industry, and I think you've got to look at the high risk of our business. It's a very fast-moving business, as you all know, and the problem is that the actual working number of days

> that you can afford to have someone in training, you know, if you're under pressure anyway, I know everyone's under pressure, but under pressure, you're making changes, whatever, and you offer them a week's training, external training, there's a highly – there's a market. You've got to keep in, in the growth part of the business. I'm not talking about the whole of it, but in the software sector you might discover that everyone is in favour, is learning [*Hm, hm*]. It's as simple as that.

Otherwise, our account of Northern Ireland's typically weak level of adult learning went almost unchallenged in the focus groups.

Northern Ireland's education system is a selective one, and one obvious possibility is that this might be connected with patterns of learning in later life. Most of the interviewees in our study were certainly convinced that selective secondary education had a significant impact on people's broader attitudes towards education. In a focus group made up of workers in the voluntary sector, a discussion started around the role of social class and adult learning. This then triggered a comment from a woman who had previously taught in a comprehensive system in Britain:

LS — And that's why class...

Cathy — Yes. And that is then cut a lot of ways, with particular issues affecting the young people, people with disability, and so on, but heavily, of course, there's the 11+, it is very heavily a class issue.

LS — Yes, the 11+, does anybody else want to take that up?

Rob — I would have thought there would be a connection. Before I went to work where I am, I actually am a qualified teacher and I taught here and over in England and I had contact with other schools as well. I am very struck by the different attitudes towards education, to the teaching, to the schools, by the pupils and by the parents as well. The pupils I have come across, they all wanted to be at a grammar school, they're just so highly motivated to get all the qualifications they could have, I can just imagine that they really would be the ones who wanted to go on and want more and more. And to some extent I just wonder do they get that at secondary school and I do feel that we do encourage attitudes by the public, we do slant public attitudes towards education by having that very final selection in the education process. I'd had a very limited experience, and that just struck me very strongly, having come from a comprehensive background in England.

Alice [organisation] works with parents and a lot of them would be young women who come to us, and recently I've thought that there's an awful lot of work we are doing virtually trying to undo the negative impressions that they have of education from when they were at school, to get them even to a point where they can consider if, for example, they want to go on to do a personal development course. It can seem quite intimidating if your impression is that education is a negative thing, and I think we need much more outreach and support if people are going to get over it, to turn back that view, even a personal development course.

Cathy This could be significant – you know, adult learning's a wide space, it covers everything doesn't it, from high-level qualifications to something such as personal development. The types of adult learning that people do are related to their previous learning experience. Well a lot of the basic education type work that Judy, myself and Anne certainly would be involved in is offering people an opportunity to bring themselves up to an educational level that schools should have got them to by the time they were about twelve. You know, an awful lot of the time has to be spent on literacy skills and numeracy skills, all that kind of – buckets and buckets of experience in, you know, work, voluntary work, all sorts of things, yet the actual education system hasn't done it, so although we're calling it adult learning it is actually reproducing a lot of work in the adult that the schools have failed do. But they haven't failed to do it with the children who have got two A Levels.

A somewhat similar comment came from a participant in the software sector focus group, who started by citing a report published by the business ginger group, Northern Ireland Growth Challenge:

Donald	They would certainly make the contention that there's this sort of vicious circle where you go to school, you get good A Levels, you go to university, you get a profession, you send your children to grammar schools, and they go round and round and round. And everybody that's inside that is fine, but anybody that's not on that merry-go-round is outside the system. I think there's a lot of truth in that, and that's why a lot of the comments that Hamill and Brian were making earlier about having difficulty in believing the percentages with regard to those that have no qualifications, that's why that view is held so widely. There is an awareness I think that there are a lot of people outside that cycle.

This issue also emerged in the rural development focus group:

Jim	... although you're saying that quite a lot of people are getting through with reasonable, um, primary qualifications, I think those that don't get to that level and don't achieve anything, I'm sure somebody who has studied them would find they'd had a very, very negative experience of the education system [*mm*]. And that certainly doesn't encourage them to want anything at all to do with any other type of education.
LS	Yes. Could we have a look at that? Because we have been talking about people with higher-level qualifications [*mm*], but there are a lot of people who haven't got those qualifications and a lot don't want to go on to any further education. How big a factor is that do you think? Have you found that it turns people off from getting involved in education?
Niall	Huge. Huge.
Joan	I've the impression it is a major factor.

Niall — If you get people together in a local history group or any community group, then you open up the box of experiences at school, it just all flows out. The, you know, the stories about the teachers, how it affected the rest of their lives, it just goes on and on and on.

Other interviewees did not name the selective system but rather pointed to what they saw as the excessively academic bent of the Northern Ireland education system. This exchange came very early on in a focus group for people working in tourism:

John — Perhaps one of the reasons why some people might say it's unlikely that they're going to continue to further their education was in fact academically they've been successful at A Level, then they have come out of a good university or college course, and they consider that that is adequate as far as education is concerned. Would that affect some of the statistics that we have?

LS — It's certainly a possibility, isn't it? It's interesting that you bring that up, certainly people in some of the other focus groups do seem to feel that there's something about Northern Ireland, that you if you do well in education and work hard, then that's it, you don't need to bother with education any further [*Mmm*].

A senior civil servant made a similar comment during the rural development focus group:

Joan — ... I do think in Northern Ireland society when you say, "Why do they not go on once they get A Levels", I think there is still an attitude here that A Levels are really equivalent to getting a degree. If you get, particularly if you get a grammar education, and you get A Levels, that's nearly as far as you need to go. I think there's still a bit of a throwback there, from that. You have really achieved something if you've got that. And if you get a job, like in the civil service through that, you really don't need to study any further. [*hubbub*] Now that is purely an observation as opposed to basing

	it on fact but I would pick that up, I feel, a lot with people.
LS	Actually, we have heard this before. Does anybody else want to comment on it? You know, the fact that there's a certain amount of complacency, a lot of people think that they've achieved a certain amount say in the grammar schools and that if you've got a secure job you don't need to go on with your education. Does that mean that we place a low value on education for its own sake?
Joan	I think we do. I do think that Northern Irish people tend to feel that, if they've gone through the normal channels – A Levels, job – what's the point, really?

One senior personnel manager in the software industry also described a similar pattern:

Janet	Well, where I would work, we're taking in graduates. It's starting at a much higher level, we're expecting a basic minimum good qualification, but after that where would I see the problem is, yes, low participation in adult learning. They feel they've done enough. It's a question of, "We don't need to go any further, we've done sufficient". So that's where I'd find an immediate fall-off. I could count on one hand the number of people that are involved in, say, distance learning or self-learning schemes.

A local economic development worker from South Armagh had a different perspective on this issue. After commenting in the rural development focus group on the high proportion of adults with no qualifications in her area, she went on:

Kate	Of more concern to us, when we actually analysed the figures of those people with qualifications, they were mainly academic, you know, theoretically-based, university degrees et cetera, and very very little on vocational qual- I nearly said 'practical' there – very little on the vocational side. Which with the high levels of unemployment, if you take the two together, we're

getting a deskilling of the workforce. And also people with the education, particularly the more academic ones, are actually leaving the area, and this is causing an even bigger gap.

Exploring this issue, participants in the tourism industry group then turned to the reasons for the dominance of academic values:

Malcolm — Right, was that because when you were going to university, leaving school, you hadn't really made up your mind what you were going to do, or was it because you didn't understand the university course you were doing?

John — I think perhaps there's this, it's a sort of a family thing, it's maybe a snob thing, it's a socioeconomic thing, that it's –

Kate — It's the thing to do, isn't it?

John — – very nice to have, yes, a degree, and I was particularly interested in this industry, and certainly it was very nice to have a good qualification. Also I must admit that because of that qualification it has helped me for example to get a part-time lecturing job and so on, and it's good on your CV.

The dominance of the academic route was generally accepted by interviewees. However, there was also discussion of how, in a divided society, religion and social class interfaced with the primacy of academic knowledge. The tourism focus group had considered this issue at the start of its meeting, but then returned to the subject later on, arguing that family aspirations had changed in the recent past, particularly among the Catholic community, and this had helped to embed the dominance of the academic route:

John — Well, it's, er, just on that point, I'm sorry to interrupt you, but I don't necessarily understand the figures in reference to GCSE. Because I think that's a socioeconomic thing, I think that's because in Northern Ireland especially there is a trend over this last 15, 20 years where socioeconomically people now, that the parents have got the chance of an education and therefore they're insisting that once again that it's a status symbol, they're insisting that their children achieve A Levels and GCSEs. That doesn't happen necessarily in Scotland, England and Wales. Northern Ireland is peculiar in that respect because there has sort of been over the years now a sort of a –

Kate – a focus on education being really important.

John Yeah, and also, well, also from a religious point of view, I hate to say it but from a religious point of view there's more emphasis on education in the Catholic community than there was in the non-Catholic community years ago, and that has made a marked difference in academic achievement at O Level or GCSE and A Level stages, so that could affect the figures slightly –

The suggestion that Catholics were more inclined towards a purely academic view of education was also made in the rural development focus group, by a Catholic professional who argued that:

Niall It's the same in the South, I'm pretty sure it is. I'm also fairly sure it is the value placed on education as a way through. I'd also be interested to look at it in terms of the sectarian divide as well. I'm not sure what you would see, but I would suspect that you would see more from Catholic backgrounds moving through that route. Because the link to the 11+ and so on in the 1947 Act was very strongly articulated within the civil rights movement, so it's embedded in the culture as the route [*um hm*]. And I suspect that vocational modes would be more akin within the Protestant community.

In the event, the survey data analysed in the next chapter showed virtually no differences in educational attitudes between the two main religious communities. However, this is by no means to downplay the importance of the academic route to the Catholic community in Northern Ireland (Black, 2004, p 70). In stark contrast to most other areas of public life, education was for most of Northern Ireland's history the one area where discrimination – at least in its more overt forms – did not place a straightforward block social on mobility.

Quite a large number of our interviewees expected that participation in adult learning would also vary by social class. The opening contribution to a focus group for voluntary sector employees came from a middle-class Catholic woman who wondered whether we could share our quantitative data with the group. The facilitator tried to deflect the question in order to steer the group back to our own agenda, but with limited success. Three minutes later, the participant returned to her original contribution:

> Gill — Coming back to my question, was it kind of geographically across the board? The reason that I asked that was that the voluntary organisations, and I imagine that for most organisations you don't need any general educational qualifications or training to join, what we find in regard to Catholic and Protestant west Belfast is that, where a lot of people aren't actually in any kind of work environment, the motivation for taking on board the learning opportunity goes, and unless you've motivated them at an early age, it's very hard to get them back into the learning environment.

And indeed Gill was right: in so far as there is any quantitative evidence on this issue, it confirms that social class is as important a factor in determining participation in adult learning in Northern Ireland as it is elsewhere (Field, 1997).

The dominance of academic values in the schools system was also held partly responsible for negative attitudes among adults, particularly those who saw themselves as educational failures. Northern Ireland's selective secondary system is ferociously competitive. In the words of one interviewee, who ran a voluntary centre in Belfast, and whose oldest child had just sat the transfer test:

> Maire — It's not just will you go to grammar, it's where you go, Methody, Academy.
>
> JF — How do people know which is the best school? How do you find that out?
>
> Maire — Everyone knows.

JF Do you talk to friends about it? League tables, that sort of thing?

Maire No. Everyone knows. You talk about the best primary, maybe, you might chat about that with the other mums. I've even, I'm already asking about Queens[4], how to get her in there. Not the grammar, there's nothing to talk about. You'd do anything to get them in.

What impact does this school-centred culture have on adults? In the focus group for managers in private sector training, the view was expressed that many adults saw courses as simply a return to schooling:

Bob The big group for us, the adults, they're really just drop-outs. That's right, isn't it. They're drop-outs and they don't see why they have to go back to class after 10 years away from class. That's what they call it, class, that's how they would see it, and they don't want it, to go back to school. It's very very difficult to bring them round.

One of the individual interviewees, who worked with ex-prisoners, spoke of the difficulty in persuading these men to continue their training at a further education college: "It's going to school for them, they see the college building down in town and it's 'school', 'teachers', it all comes back, and these are men who've been in Maghaberry, the Maze[5], for years, they've taught themselves some amazing things, and we're telling them to go to school". And if many adults see later learning as simply a return to school, then we would expect to see considerable resistance to the idea of what many people will think of as an extremely inappropriate and possibly risky activity, given their own life stage.

Even within the academic pathway, some participants suggested that a fine distinction could be made between the different tracks. A civil servant in the rural development focus group sparked off a lengthy exchange when she raised the issue of part-time higher education:

Janet Sorry, another sort of negative attitude and again it's more of an observation is that I think people don't put the same value on qualifications that have been achieved in a part-time way than those that have been achieved – say if you go to university and do, you know, your traditional three- or four-year study,

	somehow I think there's still a feeling about that that qualification must be better than one that you've done on a part-time basis. And it might be the equivalent qualification [*yeah*] but I think there's that –
JS	That's interesting, but why do you think that?
Janet	I don't know. Whether it's this feeling that because you haven't been to university as such, that because you've studied more maybe in your own time or you haven't been seen to be a university student, that you can't really be a proper graduate [laughs] or something like that.
Joan	But why, how do you feel you've had that feedback, from –?
Janet	Well, I would know say from the Open University, and I think the Open University has established itself reasonably well now, but certainly initially people who were coming forward with degrees from it were not seen to be as [*yeah*], as good. They couldn't possibly be as good as somebody who had been to, you know, a traditional university.
Joan	Yet in a sense probably more effort has been put into it.
Janet	Well, yeah, I would argue that. But at the same I don't think that's always the way it would have been seen. I think it does take a long time for people to rethink, you know, what they mean by education.

Nor did there appear to be a generally positive view of vocational training. Broad attitudes towards vocational training were reportedly still coloured by the poor reputation of 'schemes' dating back to the 1970s. As one private sector training professional put it during a focus group,

Gerry	... you can go to the schools and they would still try to talk to you about the old YTP [Youth Training Programme]. It maybe had a bad name in the schools,

teachers would maybe see it as something for the bad boys.

Expansion of tertiary education, and the proliferation of vocational qualifications, had proven something of a mixed blessing for the personnel specialists in our focus groups. An officer with the software industry federation spoke caustically of the credentialled society:

Donald — The other thing that Brian said, it's just triggered something with me, is this business about the bit of paper. I know that in my career, until comparatively recent years, on-the-job training and internal training and so on, it didn't get written down, it wasn't important, it wasn't in my CV. Nowadays one sees CVs that have pages and pages and pages of qualifications which you wouldn't look too deep, I don't want to downgrade them, but which you wouldn't really consider to be anything other than somebody's learned something that's interesting or may be a bit useful for them to know. That sort of culture has come in as a result of the implementation of quality management systems and NVQs [National Vocational Qualifications] and all that sort of thing, where anything you do there's a certificate at the end of it, some sort of documentation.

The tourism focus group also expressed real doubts about the value of vocational qualifications. This was a complex issue, as the following exchange illustrates:

John — Yeah, well, I'll be quite honest. Employers, nowadays, don't trust NVQ qualifications.

Moira — They don't.

Maureen — They don't.

John — There's been a lot of signing off of people and so on in practical situations, practical situations, and it's not properly monitored because people are taking the easy way out, because of all bookwork, they're just signing

	people off to get them through, and that's it. [*Mmm*] People can't be bothered.
Maureen	But, but, John, NVQs, all right, they've a bad name to some employers or some portions of them, but fortunately I think that it's the right way to go, because it's on-the-job [*yeah*], it's actually physical, practical training –
John	If you get it right.
Maureen	– yes, that you walk in in the morning and you can do everything connected with your job. The fact that –
LS	Is it difficult to get it right?
John	Oh, absolutely, yes.
Maureen	Because it's too bureaucratic.
John	Yeah, absolutely.
Maureen	Yeah, I mean I've looked at them, NVQs, and it's evidence is all, witnessing's all, and it's such a load of ... hassle trying to get the thing done. I think the objective of NVQs is very admirable [*yes, hmm*] and getting back to what you were saying about hands-on experience.

The private sector training industry focus group explored the question of NVQs in the context of a discussion about employers' reluctance to allow trainees to attend day release programmes:

Gill	Yes, and NVQs were supposed to get round that. You talk to any employer, they will tell you they are too expensive, NVQs are not worth the cost.
LS	NVQs are too expensive – do other people agree with that?
Richard	Well, they are costly. Employers still think –

Cathy – what's an NVQ, they have never heard of them. They still think RSA, City & Guilds, and even further back.

The bureaucracy associated with NVQs was sometimes contrasted with what people saw as the reality of actual recruitment decisions. One interviewee who worked as a police trainer, although himself involved in attempts to develop academic qualifications in policing, thought that "recruits, it isn't really qualifications you need if it's going to be someone's life that is depending on it, you're really looking for experience and character, to be honest it's something like, well, a few years in the army with a clean record, something like that". An agricultural adviser said that "Even in the processing side, they prefer someone they know, or someone that comes through someone they know. Reliability. Full stop". Some in the rural development focus group went further. One manager in a community development network, responding to a comment from a civil servant about the lack of employer support for training, announced that:

Niall You know, I suppose that what annoys me in a way is the people who have gone through the academic side and really are very ill-equipped to do jobs that you would have thought that that qualification [*um hum*] was designed for.

Informal workplace learning was the norm in all of the sectors that we studied. Even in the electronics and software industries, which recruit highly skilled specialists, there was considerable regard for informal learning. According to an interview with a sector training council officer, most of those who worked in the electronics industry were either semi-skilled operatives with Level 2 NVQs or technical specialists with qualifications at Higher National (HN) level or above: "Despite the fact that these workers held good qualifications for their respective levels, the big number who work in electronics, they probably, like get shown through their work how to do it".

A similar picture emerged from the software industry focus group, whose members recruited an almost entirely graduate (and comparatively youthful) workforce:

Brian ... you come to get a promotion and you're promoting somebody to a position, the fact that they've got an MSc is almost irrelevant in the criteria, because you know we're judging them on their practical skills. It's

> not like teaching or medicine where having extra letters after your name make a difference as to getting promotion. Even if we're recruiting experienced people, the fact that they've got an MSc would not matter a hoot after the initial take-on, because we're interested in what is their experience, how well they can do the job [*that's right*]. The fact that they've an MSc, really we'd worry that they've time on their hands and that they're academically rather than practically minded, and I'm serious on that. And the other thing we've got to define is, what is adult learning? The fact that they've completed a nine-weeks' training with [names competitor company], that's learning to me [*yes*], they're learning skills. Everybody in our industry has changed their job in the last five years fundamentally. I haven't done a professional qualification since 1980 [*no*], but I've been on one-day training courses, two-day training courses, but 90% of it's just learning by doing a different job and that is learning no matter what anybody says.

In some workplaces, informal learning was the name of the game; it was how experienced and less experienced workers alike kept abreast of new developments. By contrast, informal learning was portrayed by the tourism industry focus group as almost a subversive activity. It was necessary in order to do the job, but they believed that it was much less valued than an academic qualification. This perhaps reflected the growing pressure that the tourism industry came under in the 1990s to produce evidence for external scrutiny, as part of a government drive to improve the quality of service in an industry that it believed would benefit considerably from the peace process. Nevertheless, the group itself recognised the importance of informal learning, and one of the most vocal members of the group clearly believed that even the main vocational qualifications such as BTEC awards were of limited relevance to their own situation:

John	– with regards to whenever I left college going into my first job as an assistant manager in this industry, an awful lot of the course content was totally inapplicable and I would have been much better geared in more common sense and –
Kate	– practical –

John	– the practical business methods –
Michael	– HND, BTEC type –
John	Even further down the scale, more selected subjects like Dealing with People, Interviewing-like needs, Current Legislation – that's most important –
LS	Have you, can I just ask have you sought that?
JMcQ	Through my own trial and error.
LS	But not through looking for training?
John	No.
LS	That's interesting, so you did that deliberately, you didn't actually look for the formal education side –
John	I didn't have time, to be quite honest. First of all, initially, I was in a job and I wouldn't have had time to go ahead and look for further education. Plus the fact that my employer probably wouldn't have paid for it, all of these training courses that are available are all very expensive, and I think generally that people won't pay for them themselves, so –

A similar sense of informal learning as somehow outside the loop came from the software industry focus group. Here, though, the group quickly moved into banter, trying to punctuate the composure of one participant who argued that the focus group itself was providing him with a learning experience:

Brian	It comes back to this problem, I mean, what is adult learning? It's not just about a bit of paper. If I go on a two-day course of training, unless I get a bit of paper at the end of it, I'm sure that that doesn't come into the thinking as to what is adult learning. We're coming back to the education sector, it has to be a tech or a university or something that's giving that qualification.

Harry Brian, if I came along and asked you, do you participate in adult learning, what would the answer be?

Brian I don't but I do! [*laughter*] I would be learning all the time.

Donald If you hadn't been here today, you would have said "No" [*laughter*].

Brian See, that's just –

Donald If you hadn't have been here today, you would probably have said "No, I don't".

Brian I'm learning today. This is education for me.

Harry But if you asked that question baldly, to somebody in the street, they could well say "No", even though they had job-related training [*Yes, yes*]. That's another....

In these sectors, then, informal learning was recognised as the key way in which new skills and information were passed around. However, respondents felt that informal learning was undervalued by comparison with what they believed were the more artificial and bureaucratic standards of academic qualifications and NVQs. Informal learning was therefore held to be in a somewhat ambiguous position; in practice, though, everyone made use of it.

For those who worked in community development, informal learning was highly valued as an alternative to what were viewed as the rigidity and bureaucracy of the formal education system. The following discussion showed the value placed on conviviality as an aspect of informal learning, particularly among women; and the contrast drawn with the formal world of further and higher education (with a side swipe at one of the University of Ulster's premises in York St, Belfast). The speaker, an articulate Catholic professional with a senior position in community development, also alluded in a bantering way to the yearly Adult Learners' Week (which had taken place some weeks before the interview) and its penchant for 'celebrating adult learning'.

Niall I think the other factor is just the joy in learning. I mean, people can join in the fun, and within a culture where, you know, it's the most natural thing in the world. And I think that has been created to some extent through the women's groups, you know, where there, there is a bit of fun involved, and it's social, and so on, and you can relatively easily mix significant tasks, jobs, skills, individually, and sharing experience, and so on. It's a much broader sort of milieu, it's not the sort of classroom, the institution and so on. I think that in many ways we've got to get away from that . . .

LS Does anybody else –

Niall Well, institutionalisation. It has its place, but think I mean further education. Think of a further education college, think of a box, this horrible, ugly building. Like the Art College in York Street [*laughter*]. And it was also, I mean I did City & Guilds in woodwork and joinery, and I, it was crucifying. I mean, it was a very good experience, I'd gone through a degree and postgrad stuff, and I went back to do this and I was the oldest one in the class. It was in, in Dungannon, to be precise. It was horrifying. I mean, the way we were treated. We, it was just nothing about learning, I mean it was purely dishing out on a routine, rota basis, stuff that was so boring it was unbelievable. And I mean people did think about it as the link between their work and getting something in order to go on into joinery. I mean, that was the thought in everybody's head. Celebration of learning, anything to do with sort of opening life's theatre up, forget it [*laughter*].

Explaining the patterns

One aim of the interviews was to find out whether Northern Ireland's distinctive level and pattern of social capital might help to explain its equally distinctive pattern of divergence between initial and continuing education. As we have seen, survey data suggest that overall levels of social capital in Northern Ireland are relatively high. They also indicate that people's relationships are strongest in respect of close ties such as the immediate family, and more widely through faith organisations, including the churches. A reasonable working hypothesis was that this pattern of connections might serve to reinforce attainment in school, but that it equally might discourage behaviour by adults that might lead people to change their existing social arrangements in some way.

Both the focus groups and individual interviews provided some support for this hypothesis. Working life provides one important context for building social networks. Some of the focus group participants believed that Northern Ireland's labour market was characterised by low levels of labour mobility, which in turn discouraged employees from investing in their own development. This point was made forcibly in the software industry focus group:

Harry	Is there one other aspect in Northern Ireland? The turnover of personnel in our culture [*pretty low*] is very low [*yeah*] relative to other parts of the UK.
Brian	It *was* low.
Donald	Was low. [*laughter*]
Harry	I would say even in the IT sector, that would still be, people had jobs for life. Even in the IT sector, it would probably not be as high as it would be in other [*oh no, definitely*]. That is another element within Northern Ireland as a whole. If you could do, there's no prospect, you don't want to change your job, why train yourself up for something else? It's not the habit in Northern Ireland to change your job, whereas it might be in other parts of the country. So therefore it's not the habit to actually get yourself additional – [interruptions] – qualifications.

Subsequently, the software group debated the reasons for the low level of mobility in the local labour market. Two in particular stood out for this group: the strength of family ties (more specifically, in this example, ties to one's mother) and the dominance of government employment in the culture of the local labour market:

Brian	.... Northern Ireland is different in the economic situation, the pressure from the parents is always to get a good education and you'll be made for life. I don't think that's as strong elsewhere, across the water you'll always get a good job without education. And then secondly when you've got a job, the economic, you

	know, you don't go mucking about with that, you daren't tell your mother you're thinking of moving, "Sure you've got a good job, and you're there for life, you stay there". I think that's part of the psyche that's in us, and I still think it's being inculcated into us.
Donald	That's the PPP, you've got a permanent pensionable post [*yep*], that my mother used to talk about [*yes*].
LS	Do you think that most people feel that that's a thing of the past?
Harry	Mm, there's still a very high number of people employed by government, and the government posts are PPP. [*well*] Even now, even now. I think most people consider that if you've got a job in the civil service, you're there for life.
Donald	It's a lot more secure than most jobs in the private sector.
Harry	You'd better believe it. [*laughter*]

The culture of public sector employment was also alluded to in the rural development focus group. One community worker from County Down commented that:

Niall	The other thing, in our area we're sort of, Belfast would be the biggest pull. And the type of work that is generally available to, even with five O Levels, would be a queue for civil service type and that type of work and there's very little pressure on a lot of those lower grades that they develop or improve qualifications. That may be part of the problem down our way, and they hope they're in for life once they're in.

In other areas, labour mobility might mean short-term migration or long-distance commuting. In South Armagh, it was claimed, the demand for unskilled labour from the Republic was also depressing the demand for skills training:

Kevin — Yeah, there's no employment opportunities [*yeah*]. The market doesn't value what they can offer. Therefore they're going to Dublin, where the market does value, they get the correct rate for the job. I mean, you would be talking about earning three or four times there what they would earn say in South Armagh, and therefore why bother getting the higher grade which would pay them the rate at home when you can travel and get it somewhere else [*yes*]. And England traditionally fulfilled that market place where they were getting value for their basic qualifications in the construction industry.

Dan — Yeah, we have industry that's competing on the basis of low wages, and that does not value the individual or the individual's contribution [*mm*]. It just values the minimum task again that they do.

Even here, though, workers commuted to Dublin on a daily or weekly basis, rather than leaving South Armagh for a new home in the South.

A general reluctance to move in search of work was widely acknowledged in the focus groups – perhaps surprisingly so, given that Northern Ireland in fact has quite a high rate of emigration. The following exchange in the rural development focus group, initiated by a civil servant, suggests that a number of factors are seen as operational:

Janet — Now, I don't think we should be afraid of people leaving. I think this sort of attitude that we can only educate people to have jobs and sit around Ireland for the rest of their lives, I think is a very inhibiting sort of attitude to have. I think, you know, people going away and some coming back, as a lot of them do, I think is a much more healthy way to look at it. And therefore I don't think people should be as I say sort of falling into this thing where there's no jobs at home here so therefore you only look at what you can possibly do to stay here. And that –

Kevin — – It's very hard to sell that, though!

Janet — But I think, I think that can be [*yes*], that is certainly a problem, certainly from a training point of view which

I can talk about, where I would have experience in a village where you just couldn't get people to see that there would be jobs but they would have to move away from home [*of course, yeah*]. You know, sometimes that move was, it mightn't be more than 20 miles, but that was just too much for them to go.

As noted above, a preference for informal learning was far more common, combined with a reliance on interpersonal connections to help inform decisions about recruitment and selection.

Personal connections and reputation counted for a lot, as is illustrated in this discussion of NVQs in the software industry focus group:

Brian	But again I think we have to just, it matters if people are learning, not as much that they do get paper qualifications for it. It doesn't concern us in Northern Ireland on that at all.... We as an organisation do give people NVQs, but the big difficulty with NVQs is the whole documentation side. NVQ is about 75% paperwork, just for the sake of proving something. Practically we're not interested in that. We know ourselves if we've put somebody through a training course, and they know themselves they've got that skill. But to get an NVQ you've got to quadruple the cost of getting it. I think that whole thing has spoilt it for the industry as far as I'm concerned, and that's wearing a number of hats [*mmm*].

So for this speaker, entry-level qualifications might be significant on initial appointment, but subsequently personal knowledge was more significant:

Brian	Early, getting the good degree is the important point at getting you started. After that practical ability, proving you can do the job more than qualifications, which –
LS	Yes. How do you assess that when you're employing people? How do you assess that they've got the abilities that they need in the job?
Brian	We'd be looking for them to poach [*laughter*].

Similar observations arose in the public sector healthcare focus group:

David There's a personal observation. I've no hard evidence for it, but in a small area like Northern Ireland there's perhaps not the same level of mobility in your career. Now, if you're being mobile in your career, you're applying for a job, they've never heard of you, so the qualifications are very important, they sort of identify you. If you're living in a bigger area, say England or Scotland, the need for your career progression, I've no evidence but experience, but it may well depend to a higher level on your academic progression than here in Northern Ireland where your competency or the way people talk about you, you know, "He or she did a good job", um, that may play [*uh huh*] a much stronger role [*that's true*]. If that's the case, then we're back to the employers and their attitudes where being seen to do a good job is more important than being quali-, getting extra qualifications.

Moreover, personal connections could be used as a way of influencing the education system. When the software focus group was meeting, participants were anticipating a significant skills gap as a result of continued expansion in the industry. In the event, the collapse of the dot.com bubble relaxed the squeeze on a tight labour market. However, when we met, the industry was worried that too few graduates would be coming through, and that resources would need to be diverted into upskilling. Initially, attempts had been made to resolve the problem through personal contacts:

LS Is there enough communication between the industry and the universities? Is that situation discussed?

Donald There probably isn't, to be honest about that. Certainly the views that Brian has expressed, they have been expressed to the people within the IT departments, to people like [name of senior IT academic] and so on, and to their equivalents at Queen's. I think that they recognise that and there have been changes. But they also are in a situation where they are capped on funding and all that sort of thing, which makes it more difficult for them to react. I think that there is a genuine gap here which the private sector will probably fill itself. I don't necessarily believe that educating people is the sole parameter of the universities or the colleges of further education. I mean, that's an area too where there's big scope for bringing people through the system in the further and higher education colleges. There's an opportunity too to work with them.

There was also widespread recognition of the importance of networks and associations as factors that could increase demand for learning. A South Armagh man commented during the rural development focus group that:

Kevin — Usually, the first couple of meetings of a new community group, education will be right up there, very much at the top of the agenda, particularly for those who are organising or committee members. They will be quite open about their lack of educational qualifications or experience in the field.... Certainly in Newry, the Communities in Action ones that went through that programme first were more confident than the ones that didn't go on it, and dropped off the committee and haven't participated in any sense. Even the smaller one, the Ulster People's College community leadership programme, it's starting to get more and more people involved and valuing going back to education and training.

Public sector employment was viewed as the only area where studying for a qualification as an adult might make sense. Some members of the tourism focus group believed that formal qualifications were required to progress one's career both within government agencies, and within the semi-public bodies financed by one of Northern Ireland's many external funding agencies:

John — With respect, why do you need a Masters? Because you are articulate, obviously successful in your job, I would imagine that you can be quite persuasive if you put your mind to it [*laughter*].

Kate — Well, I will need a Masters' degree to move up another level....

John	And will you be able to apply it?
Maureen	But, John, applying it is immaterial in a way. It's proof of something, and as well as that it's a way of sifting people out when an advert goes in the paper. They can put down a Masters, it requires an MA –
Moira	This is so. The government jobs, NITB[6], we're getting away from the industry as such.
Kate	There's certainly something in that, it's not just the government, any job that's being funded by an organisation, whether it's the International Fund for Ireland, the Tourist Board or anybody – my job is funded – and you have to have had a degree to get it.

But this was an exception.

Family was sometimes cited in the interviews as a cause of low demand for learning. Women in particular appeared to come under pressure from other family members to look after their own children, and fit any work around the primary task of child-rearing. Unlike other barriers to learning, which were mentioned for both women and men, it is unlikely to come as a surprise that child-rearing was only ever mentioned in the case of women. According to a male professional in the rural development focus group,

Niall	... there is a lot of reasons why people don't, why women in particular don't go, try to improve themselves academically.
LS	Okay, can we look at that for a moment? Why is that, would you say? [*silence*] Presumably issues to do with childcare, and –
Niall	Very good, very good, cost of childcare is number one. Lack of family support, low salaries is an issue in the tourism type of area that we live in as well, poor public transport and the cost of that, lack of skill, lack of experience, fear of the unknown and intimidation, fear of change, lack of local employment opportunities, lack of flexibility in employment, school holidays – a big issue with women, generally, and quality of

childcare, as well as quality of childcare there's the cost, lack of childcare options, and a reluctance to leave children with strangers.

A female professional, and Protestant, endorsed this view of the woman as the primary child rearer, but suggested that this was also an opportunity:

Janet — I think another reason, I'm not sure if this would support what Niall's study was, women also see their role very much as encouraging their children to learn. And I think that they feel that maybe in their younger years they haven't achieved but now they need to. I think that, certainly again I think from my own experience with literacy education, that certainly was a big factor in a lot of women returning there. I think it can help, it can have an impact in other situations as well too.

On the other hand, some participants believed that women were more likely than men to respond positively to the challenges of change. A male Catholic professional in the rural development focus group aired this issue in the context of a comment on the value of informal learning:

James — Then there is also the link between the informal and the formal. If you get involved in the informal you're more likely to get into the formal than you would if you don't. And then I think the vocational would attract more men. I think that the gender thing is a real issue, a huge issue. And my sense is there'd be a much greater appetite among women to get back into education than there is with the men.

LS — Why should that be?

James — I think the whole issue of change and the whole issue, um.... Women expect, um ... that they have to fight to get any place, men expect it to be more laid out. Men get work, men provide for the family et cetera, maybe it isn't the way it is any more, the fact that that doesn't happen.... Also just to admit that you don't know things is harder for men.

So interviewees identified a wide range of cultural issues that, they believed, served as disincentives to learning in adult life.

As well as such cultural factors, there was also recognition that the structure of the local economy tended to reduce demand for adult learning. According to two women in the tourism industry focus group,

Maureen	There could be a degree of cynicism then, once you've left school and you get a job, you're in a job, maybe that's you for life. There's a more cynical attitude, perhaps it's to do with the Troubles.
Kate	It's more an attitude. A lot of people leave school at an early age in Northern Ireland, and go to work for small family firms. They don't have the opportunity to go and work for multinationals or national companies, that require them furthering their education, that have the kind of size that would lead them to hold internal training courses for their workers, that would have career guidance paths, that would have promotional opportunities. There are an awful lot of people who have come out of school in Northern Ireland with very very good qualifications, people who were at school with me and are now working in shops and offices, and they don't have any opportunity of training.

The facilitator then probed further into the group's views on the dominance of small firms in the local tourism industry:

LS	Small businesses, is it more a small business or a family business?
John	Family, yeah [*Ah, mmm*].
LS	And what is the attitude in the family businesses towards training in the family?
Kate	[*Laughter*] Keep it in the family!
Maureen	Cut costs [*Yeah*].

John	That's a very valid point. Cut costs. I have training, in hospitality, at [name of training centre], and you know there are something like eighty training courses and so on there. I have a look, one day course, £125, and so on, it's all expensive. And so you've got [*sure*] the cost of time of sending those people away [*absolutely*] and you can't afford the manpower, you're really stretched, you can't afford to send people off, and you can't afford to pay for the course. They aren't self-motivated, they won't pay for it themselves, their expectation is that their employer is the one that's going to be paying.

Even the availability of grant aid for training was, it seems, insufficient to persuade small business people to abandon their reliance on informal modes of recruitment and training. As a local government tourism development officer put it:

Maureen	... some of the NITB grants for the development of facilities, I also work on a marketing course where there's huge resentment of trying to teach your granny to suck eggs, and there's people who won't take the money, there's one or two -
John	Don't want to know.
LS	Why is there resentment?
Maureen	They feel they're in the job, they've been doing it for 20 years.
Moira	Think they know it all. It's a bit like this, "I came up, I've got no training at all and I'm running the business, and I'm making this nice happy living, thank you very much, to put in an extra 10 bedrooms why should I take a marketing course or why should I take a whatever?"...
LS	So they're saying that going on this course, going on training, it's not going to help you, it's not going to make you more money. Is that a problem of attitude, or –

Moira	It probably is an inherent criticism of the system, in that they feel that the people who do the training don't know the real world.
Maureen	They haven't the respect for the course or maybe for the people running the course.

Here, then, an industry dominated by small firms was seen as typically peopled by hard-headed entrepreneurs whose experience of the world clashed with the well-meaning but naïve intentions of policy makers and academics. The consequence was an occupational culture that viewed formal training and education with some cynicism.

The private sector trainers were preoccupied with quite a different structural barrier. For this group, the benefits system was to blame for creating a significant drag. This issue was discussed repeatedly in this focus group, but the following exchange will give a taste of their unanimity:

Richard	Benefits are higher than wages, yes, they can be for some people. If you have children.
LS	Is that other people's experience as well?
Cathy	Yes.
Una	Yes.
George	Yes.

The private sector trainers returned to this topic when prompted by a question about the New Deal (which was being spoken of at the time as Welfare to Work):

Richard	That's the reality at the coalface. We are the ones who have to face them and try to get them to do something useful for once. It isn't all doom and gloom, you do have the ones that you feel are the success stories. But some of them, they will, they will come in because they have been sent there and they will start to wreck the place.
Harry	They get stuck in a rut, they can't get out of it.

Gill — Especially the young ones who are caught in the benefits trap. By the time their children have left home, they have forgotten how to go out of the house and communicate with other people. We get them, you really cannot do much with them.

Here, we see one more group of experienced professionals whose occupational common sense is that training in isolation is simply a charade.

Finally, there was the impact of 30 years of the Troubles. Several local development workers believed that the Northern Ireland conflict had created a widespread sense of powerlessness, and some argued that this was compounded by distance between the political authorities and the people. The following exchange was initiated by an economic development worker – male and Catholic – from South Armagh, and followed up by a rural educator – female and Protestant – from Mid-Ulster:

Kevin — ... If you don't have local people in charge of the future running of this, if it's every couple of years wait for the Secretary of State to put their foot in their mouths before they're out again [*laughter*], you know, that is not a tribute to a stable economy. And I mean Baroness Denton [Minister for Northern Ireland] was trying to say last year that she felt some sort of stake in society [*laughter*], and it rang so hollow that even if she meant it quite sincerely and genuinely that she wanted to see the state improve, she wanted to see it competitive, and run it, and I think that it was very sincere, but what can you do when you're somebody who's not appointed by local people? There was no power there, there was no authority to take forward radical steps and to reorganise departments.... And it's largely been because of the fact that we have been ruled from out-of-state and have never had that authority, never had that responsibility and while the European grants are still there that mentality will always be there, of let's be as conservative as possible, let's just keep the minimum standard, and we'll get by because there'll always be the grants coming out of government.

Joan — I couldn't agree more strongly with that, because there is no local accountability here. And if there is no local accountability and if people aren't learning how to become confident and how to have faith in their own abilities to effect change, then they are going to be not motivated to take up a lot of the opportunities that present themselves.

However, this was almost immediately challenged by another speaker in the same group, who drew attention to the importance of the European Commission's attempts to involve local authorities and voluntary organisations in decision making through its special initiative for peace and reconciliation.

James — Well, I think that maybe if, um, I mean, you have to look at where things are moving, what sort of trends. So if, actually, the Peace and Reconciliation Programme are moving decision making down, and are trying to implicate more people, and that's being productive, then let's, um, try to begin [to] move that further. Are the educational links, we need a much more strong educational links to that process that would make it better or more effective. I think it's important to look at that. What is the link between education and people taking more responsibility for their own lives and beginning to get engaged? At least, I don't know, but I suspect we haven't explored sufficiently what the opportunities are there, and the importance of that at the local level.

At this time, however, the European Community's special initiative was still in its early stages, and the uncertain benefits of devolved government were still in the future.

Generally, people saw the Troubles as having had a rather ambiguous impact on adult learning. In the focus group for private sector trainers, this became a source of dark banter between a male Protestant who ran a training centre in North Belfast and a female Catholic who managed a similar centre in Lisburn:

Richard — But, well, then you have the other side of it, Belfast, gaol has been an influence. Some people come out of gaol, you can say they have become an active learner, very active learner! You have all these women's groups in Belfast as well, they are very active, there are a lot of them. You don't have men's groups, though, just women's groups –

Cathy — West Belfast, they would be very genned up on courses now, especially the women's groups. They do a lot of education. They might start with something, building confidence or something, then they go on, progress.

Richard — – and the Shankill. But there are surveys, this survey showed there's a lot of people in West Belfast have never accessed a programme –

Cath — – they must all be on the Shankill then [*laughter*], the classes are all full on the Falls. Very parochial. There was this centre, on the news, people wouldn't travel even a hundred yards –

Richard — – "a stone's throw" away [*laughter*].

Otherwise, the impact of Northern Ireland's divisive political legacy was largely viewed as negative. While there was recognition of the powerful impulse to learn that could be inspired by the issues that had given rise to Northern Ireland's lengthy conflict, this was more than counterbalanced by the tendencies towards fatalism and alienation that it had engendered. According to an economic development worker from South Armagh,

Kevin — ... there's some very, very anecdotal stuff about people getting involved in paramilitary violence and getting involved in education and training and employment. And I know it's very, very hard to prove that. Purely for a community's stability, that if you have a learning community that maybe values those, even if it's a way out of the community, it's still a value base. And in the worst of our housing estates the figures are so bad that it proves that there's no value in employment, there's no value in education, and therefore what are the alternatives? And if you add onto that a whole sort of idea of alienation maybe towards the state, unless you can start changing things from the bottom up, you know, it's just window dressing. We're doing more and more of it, it's becoming more and more popular, and it now tends to be women taking the lead, particularly

> through the Workers' Educational Association approach where more and more people are getting in and they are valuing education and that's great stuff. But the most marginalised and people who are affected the most by violence are not getting involved at any level.

The risks of moving away from local neighbourhoods, particularly in areas affected most directly by the civil conflict, were cited by one of the private sector trainers, who was speaking in a focus group held during a period of cease-fire:

> Hilary — Have we taken account of the Troubles? I would say especially with evening class, for a long time people were not going out at night. You didn't like to leave your home at night. I think that might be still the case for some people, too.
>
> LS — I think that is a good point.
>
> Richard — It is a good point.
>
> Hilary — I would think it has a bearing on –
>
> Richard — That's true. Not just at night, either, you wouldn't go into certain areas any time of the night or day.
>
> Hilary — – people's experience. Yes, not just for evening classes and perhaps for training. Also jobs. You would be careful about where you took a job. You wouldn't take a job here or take one there because it might mean trouble or something. . .
>
> Richard — Mobility here is very little. You don't move far. We are a bit parochial maybe.
>
> Hilary — Yes, but I remember times, check points or trouble somewhere, people would maybe not have any idea how long it would take them to get to work. You might, if there was a checkpoint, it might take forty minutes just [*yes*]. And that's before you think about the rest of the journey.

On balance, then, the interviewees felt that the Troubles were among the factors that had damaged lifelong learning. Virtually everyone was aware of the self-education programmes for prisoners, particularly perhaps Republican prisoners, and of the remarkable achievements of some of the community-based groups, especially women's groups, in those neighbourhoods that had witnessed the worst violence. On balance, though, they thought that the Troubles had created immediate practical barriers, and also helped to generate a wider culture that was at best indifferent and at worst actively hostile to learning.

Social capital and human capital: complementary or substitutes?

This part of the analysis suggests that social capital does indeed play a part in respect of both formal and informal learning. However, it suggests that it plays differing roles in respect of formal and informal learning, and also that its impact varies at differing stages of the life cycle. In respect of formal learning, it is clear that there is a strong communal consensus around the value of academic qualifications. Family enforces this consensus, but so does much of the wider community, so that children are strongly encouraged by those around them to conform and perform at school. In respect of initial learning, the qualitative evidence suggests that people in Northern Ireland actively use their social capital resources to promote high levels of formal achievement among young people. As Coleman suggested, then, social capital and human capital complement one another, at least in this respect.

In adult life, the picture is much less certain. We have seen from the interview evidence that the main factor in securing a new position is likely to be one's reputation, triangulated through the opinions of others who are known to the person making the decision. Reputation and personal knowledge of someone's capacity, as they have demonstrated through practice over time, are also highly significant in other appointment decisions, such as promotions. In adult life, the family seems more likely to play the role of a brake on personal development and change, which might otherwise threaten the stability and continuity of community life. People acquire new skills and knowledge, and create new understandings, through interaction with known others, in settings – family, workplace, neighbourhood – that seem to be characterised by high levels of stability. Thus in adult life, we appear to find that social capital can provide a substitute for human capital.

The findings of the qualitative study therefore broadly support a qualified version of the substitution hypothesis. Rather than complementing one another, as Coleman predicted for schoolchildren, adults can adopt strategies based on their social ties to substitute very effectively for investment in human capital. Only by redefining human capital investments so as to include informal learning along with such formal indicators as certification and years of schooling can we see the two as generally complementary. Broadening the concept of human capital in this way, however desirable conceptually, would of course render it virtually unusable for those economists who prefer the clarity of an easily measurable concept to the muddle of one that corresponds to a messy reality. Northern Ireland is, of course, a very particular place with very distinctive forms of social organisation, and with strong institutions that embody very close ties, buttressed by the shared sets of values that are characteristic of faith-based communities. It is important not to generalise too much from this particular instance. However, the data presented above do seem to demonstrate that for many purposes, information acquired informally through connections, and skills picked up from workmates and family, can be far more effective in certain circumstances than those transmitted by formal educational institutions. This is an important finding, and one that may potentially have considerable wider significance. The following chapter goes on to find out how far social capital can be seen as a fundamental influence on adult learning.

Notes

[1] Although Scotland took part in PISA 2000, the Scottish Executive chose to implement the survey slightly differently, so that comparisons with England and Northern Ireland must be treated with caution.

[2] It can be argued that Scotland has a higher proportion entering higher education (HE), on the basis of official statistics that include short-cycle HE in further education colleges. However, not only do these include some very short programmes indeed, but they are also generally characterised by low completion rates (see Field, 2004).

[3] Interviews' names are anonymised. Lynda Spence (LS) served as facilitator for the focus groups; she and I (JF) conducted the individual interviews.

[4] Queen's University Belfast.

[5] Prisons, then catering almost exclusively for long-term prisoners.

[6] Northern Ireland Tourist Board.

THREE

Social connections and adult learning: survey evidence

The interview evidence suggests that the link between social engagement and lifelong learning is a complex one. The idea that social capital and human capital always pull together, which can be found in both Putnam's and Coleman's work, is simply not tenable in the light of the qualitative evidence presented in the previous chapter. People sometimes treat networks as an alternative to participation in learning, and sometimes they undertake informal learning by mobilising their social capital resources. In Northern Ireland, with its strong networks of close ties, it seems that participation in formal adult learning can sometimes be hindered by the very same social networks that foster informal learning. Close ties can function to support schools in socialising the young, but they can also provide alternatives to education and training for adults, and they can foster a culture of cynicism and disengagement from formal learning among adults.

At the individual level, and at the level of the community, the relationship between social networks and adult learning is a complex one in which people actively develop learning identities and strategies that enable them to tackle the circumstances in which they find themselves. However, what the qualitative findings did not make clear was whether people who are active in their community are more or less likely to be positive about adult learning. This chapter presents quantitative data, taken from a major social attitudes survey conducted in 2000 and 2001. The Northern Ireland Life and Times Survey (NILTS) was launched in 1998, and is the successor to the Northern Ireland counterpart of the British Social Attitudes Survey[1]. The data presented here come largely from a module on lifelong learning, although they have been analysed in conjunction with responses to questions about cultural and community life.

In general, the questions were addressed to people's attitudes rather than their behaviour, but they are helpful to the purpose of this study because the attitudes can be taken as reflecting more broadly the values shared by respondents, as well as providing valuable insights in their own right. The core idea of social capital is the suggestion that people's connections have value because they allow people to cooperate for mutual benefit, and gain access to resources that they can then use. A preliminary study suggested that this general insight could be applied to the understanding of patterns of participation in learning (Schuller and Field, 1998). The survey data allow for a more systematic and evidence-based review of this proposition, and should also allow us to find out whether people who are more engaged in their community are more or less positive in their attitudes towards adult learning than people who are less engaged. However, before going on to consider the data from NILTS, a brief summary of other survey data should help to set the scene.

Social capital and lifelong learning: a positive cycle?

The previous chapter suggested that dense networks in Northern Ireland appeared in many circumstances to substitute for participation in learning. These rather complicated findings are at odds with some of the existing survey evidence, which suggests pretty straightforwardly that people who are sociable are more likely to be doing some learning. These are the headline findings from the 2002 omnibus survey of adult learning in the UK (Field, 2003b), and they are of course highly relevant to the continuing discussion about community and participation in what has steadily become a highly individualised society. In broad terms, these survey data suggest that people who are involved in their community are more likely to be adult learners than those who are less involved; people who go out frequently for their leisure are also more likely to participate in learning; conversely, though, people whose leisure interests revolve around their home are, on the whole, less likely to be adult learners. So, at this general statistical level, there seems to be a reasonably close association between adult learning and civic engagement.

The 2002 survey contained a number of questions that were designed to shed light on the relationship between social capital and adult learning. These questions can be grouped into three broad areas. First, it included questions about people's main leisure interests, which covered a number of activities that were likely to involve associations with other people (including voluntary service, attendance at a place of worship, participation in sporting activity and socialising with others), as well as activities that focused more on the home (such as gardening). Second, it asked about frequency of engagement in a number of activities, some of which were associated with higher levels of interaction with others (including attendance at cinemas, community centres and places of worship). Third, it posed a question about people's general levels of trust. This question was taken from the World Values Survey; while it only offers a very crude indicator of trust, the responses might indicate whether this dimension of social capital is worth further study. This chapter draws on the responses to all three sets of questions.

The first clear finding from the 2002 adult learning survey was that people who are more connected with others are more likely to be adult learners. In analysing the responses, I divided people's leisure interests into those that are largely home-based and those involving a high level of interaction with others. Those that intrinsically require people to interact with others were attending a place of worship, taking part in social activities (family, friends, disco, eating out, pub and so on), participating in sports (including keep-fit and walking), performing music, and lastly volunteering and committee work. Do-it-yourself (in this survey including handicrafts), indoor games, knitting and sewing, and gardening were all defined as typically home-based activities for the purposes of this analysis.

In all those interests involving a high level of interaction with others, the survey found that participants were more likely than the population at large to be adult learners. Levels of current and recent learning were above the national average for people involved in attending a place of worship, taking part in social activities, participating in sports, performing music, and volunteering and committee work. In each case, those involved in high levels of interaction were also less likely to describe themselves as never having done any learning than were the general population.

The picture is somewhat more complex when it comes to home-based interests. In two cases, participants were more likely than average to be learners: people interested in DIY/handicrafts are likely to be current/recent learners, as are people interested in indoor games. In the case of people playing indoor games, it could be argued that theirs is an activity that is home-based, but not isolated. Most indoor games require a partner, and sometimes several, so the finding here is consistent with the general association between connectedness and adult learning. In the other two cases – knitting/sewing and gardening – people are much less likely to report current/recent learning, and come in at well under the average for the population at large. Both these interests are not only based in the home, they also do not require any interaction with others and can be undertaken in isolation (it is sometimes said that people prefer to spend time in their garden for precisely this reason).

These findings are broadly consistent with the general hypothesis of a positive association between social capital and participation in adult learning. In terms of the language adopted so far, they support the complementarity thesis rather than the substitution thesis. This impression is further strengthened by findings from the same survey, which show that not only are people more likely to be learners if they take an interest in sociable activities, those who spend most time on those activities are also more likely to learn than those who spend no time on them. While some of these activities might be thought directly to complement learning (such as visiting a library), others are likely to compete with it (such as visiting the cinema). Thus, the results to these questions are important because frequent participation in an activity must consume time and resources that cannot then be used for other activities, including learning. Yet, the findings suggest that going out and learning do not compete – on the contrary, they are strongly associated with one another.

Finally, the 2002 adult learning survey suggests that the most outgoing people tend to do different kinds of learning from those who go out less often. Among learners who are also frequent cinema goers, for example, the most common reasons for study are personal development and educational progression; they are also more likely to be working for a qualification than not. Those who rarely visit a cinema, by contrast, are much more likely to be studying as a result of somebody else's decisions, or for work reasons; they are less likely to be studying for a qualification. A slightly different pattern emerges among those who visit social clubs/ community centres. Once again it is those who go least frequently who are most likely to say their learning was "not my choice" or, to a lesser extent, is related to work, but there is no difference between frequent visitors and others as to whether they study for qualifications. In the case of places of worship, it is learners who visit occasionally (less than once a week to once a month) who are most likely to be studying as a result of somebody else's decisions. The most frequent attendees are more likely to be working for qualifications, while those who rarely or never attend are more likely not to be aiming for qualifications.

These findings suggest a degree of complexity in people's learning careers, in which lifestyle, age and social position intersect with degree of social engagement to produce particular patterns of participation. Yet, one consistent pattern appears from the data: those who are engaged in the most active social and cultural lives are also the most likely to be in control of their own learning, and to be doing their learning for educational and personal reasons.

One obvious question is whether the converse also follows: in other words, are isolated people less likely to be learners? This is suggested by the example of gardeners, many of whom apparently enjoy their favoured activity in isolation from others. There are also other highly suggestive findings elsewhere in the survey; the questions on life transitions show that some particular circumstances are strongly associated with non-participation in learning, while other changes appear to favour participation. Some of these are obvious and predictable; for example, serious illness is very strongly associated with non-learning, while the loss of a job shows a small association with learning (often, equally predictably, undertaken because of another person's decision). However, what is also striking is that retirement and bereavement, both of which remove people from key sources of social support, are associated with much lower levels of participation than average. By contrast, the end of a relationship with a partner is closely and positively associated with much higher levels of participation. It is tempting to speculate on precisely why people who split up with their partner are more likely to learn, but in this context it is perhaps best left for further investigation.

The main finding from the 2002 adult learning survey was, importantly, that, in general, adult learners mainly tend to be joiners, and vice versa. This is a much more positive finding, and a more straightforward one, than the complex picture of substitution that emerged from the qualitative data. Interestingly, too, it was also broadly the pattern that emerged from the NILTS data.

Findings from NILTS

This section presents survey evidence of people's attitudes towards learning in adult life, and how these vary among people engaged in different types of organised civic activity. In examining this empirical evidence, I am hoping to explore the nature of the relationships between engagement in civic activity on the one hand and attitudes towards adult learning on the other. Like any other source of data, NILTS is of course very limited in what it can tell us; the results nonetheless demonstrate clear differences in attitude between those who are engaged in a particular civic activity and those who are not active. Significantly, and unexpectedly, they also indicate a marked divergence among different groups of the inactive. Through this detailed examination, the aim is to contribute to our wider understanding of the role of adult learning in promoting participation and inclusion in a modern social order.

Initially designed to provide a localised component of the British Social Attitudes Survey, NILTS is carried out annually and documents public opinion on a wide range of social issues. The 2001 survey, in which 1,800 adults were questioned, contained modules on lifelong learning and on social capital[1]. In summary, the survey found that the adult population in Northern Ireland held overwhelmingly positive views of lifelong learning. This consensus was shared more or less equally across all social classes, all age groups, both genders and all three main faith communities (in other words, Catholic, Protestant, and none). While there were some minor differences between the Catholic and the Protestant populations in terms of their broad value sets (with Protestants tending towards slightly more individualistic standpoints, and Catholics marginally more supportive of welfarist approaches), these were very limited. Slightly greater differences were found by age group, as well as by such familiar factors as social class and initial educational experience. These differences were more or less as might have been predicted; for example, manual workers and the least qualified were marginally less positive in their overall attitudes towards lifelong learning, and – together with older people – most likely to feel themselves powerless to respond to technological change. But these variations should be seen as differences within a broad and widely shared consensus, which in general showed very few differences across different parts of the population.

Simplistic stereotypes about the main religious communities are also confounded by the results of the social capital module (Murtagh, 2002). Brendan Murtagh contradicts much local conventional wisdom in showing that, for most activities, Protestants appear to be more active than Catholics, particularly with respect to clubs, societies and church-based activities; participation in purely social activity was more finely balanced. NILTS also found that a considerable level of activity takes place in a mixed religion environment; mixing is, perhaps predictably, selective with respect to social class and geography, with the most mixed activities being undertaken by those from the top two socioeconomic categories. By contrast, over half of all soccer players played mainly within their own neighbourhood, and only 31% in a mixed religion setting. Murtagh concludes that, for the most affluent and mobile, new identities are being formed around lifestyles and consumption patterns that are disembedded from the traditional ethno-religious identity structures of Northern Ireland, while the effects of segregation and everyday fear continue to reinforce these identities among less advantaged groups.

While this seems a reasonable conclusion to draw from the survey, the findings also tell us much about the nature of social capital in Northern Ireland. First, as already noted, they suggest that overall stocks are relatively high. The survey confirms other studies in showing that overall levels of civic engagement in Northern Ireland are notably higher than in Britain. Yet, NILTS also suggests that much of the difference with Britain – although not all – is accounted for by what look like archetypal forms of bonding capital: family, close friends/neighbours and traditional church – and of course these features are closely intertwined, with church membership passing down through the family. It is also important to note Murtagh's point about the segregated nature of social capital among much of the working class and, above all, the most disadvantaged, who may rarely venture far from their own neighbourhood. It seems that Northern Ireland is socially divided, not along the simple two-religions model of popular stereotypes, but between an increasingly cosmopolitan and financially comfortable middle class, who tend to intermingle across sectarian divides, and a more inward-looking and possibly defensive pattern of life in working-class communities, which tend to be much more segregated.

The qualitative research suggested that this general pattern was also associated with relatively low levels of participation in formal adult education and training, partly because dense networks of close ties provide effective informal means of exchanging information, skills and ideas. NILTS complements this earlier work by allowing a quantitative analysis of the association between attitudes towards types of civic engagement and aspects of lifelong learning. The findings reported here are selected from a much larger body of data, and have been chosen mainly because they appear to shed light on the links between social capital and lifelong learning. In particular, I focus on attitudes towards four specific types of engagement: (a) community, or neighbourhood-based groups; (b) cultural activities; (c) churches and other faith-based organisations; and (d) sports. These are then related to people's attitudes towards lifelong learning.

At the most general level, the NILTS findings broadly confirm the picture given in the adult learning survey, suggesting a clear positive association between attitudes favouring lifelong learning and affirmative attitudes towards all four forms of engagement. In saying this, it is important to note that this generally positive consensus appears to command majority support from all parts of the population, including all the main religious groups. Indeed, as in so many other areas of social life, attitudes towards lifelong learning showed relatively little variation between the main religious groups. This contrasts with the marked divergence of attitudes that were found between the different social classes (with the middle class showing much higher levels of positive attitudes towards lifelong learning), and previous educational experience (with the better educated generally being the most positive).

As might be expected on the basis of the 2002 adult learning survey and other existing research, general attitudes towards lifelong learning were more positive among those who saw civic engagement as important. However, Tables 3.1-3.4 also show a clear association between positive attitudes towards lifelong learning and negative attitudes towards each of the four forms of engagement. This apparently paradoxical association between positive attitudes towards lifelong learning and negative attitudes towards engagement is, though, rather weaker than the association between positive attitudes and active engagement. Positive attitudes towards lifelong learning were weakest, by contrast, among those who thought each form of engagement was "neither important nor unimportant" to their own lives.

Table 3.1: Percentage agreeing with statement: "Learning in later life opens up a whole new world for people"

Importance of own participation in community activities (OWN LEIS2)	Strongly agree/agree
Important	93.8
Neither	77.2
Not important	83.5

Table 3.2: Percentage agreeing with statement: "Learning in later life opens up a whole new world for people"

Importance of own participation in cultural events (OWN LEIS3)	Strongly agree/agree
Important	94.4
Neither	77.0
Not important	83.7

Table 3.3: Percentage agreeing with statement: "Learning in later life opens up a whole new world for people"

Importance of own participation in church activities (OWN LEIS4)	Strongly agree/agree
Important	90.1
Neither	67.7
Not important	86.5

Table 3.4: Percentage agreeing with statement: "Learning in later life opens up a whole new world for people"

Importance of own participation in sports (OWN LEIS1)	Strongly agree/agree
Important	90.6
Neither	75.3
Not important	84.1

In short, within the overall consensus on lifelong learning, there is a marked bipolar effect with the highest levels of positive attitudes being found among those who are most positive about civic engagement, but they are followed closely by those who are actively negative about those same forms of civic engagement. Those who are undecided about civic engagement show the least positive attitudes towards lifelong learning.

The survey also explored people's attitudes towards lifelong learning and citizenship. More specifically, it asked respondents whether they thought lifelong learning made people better citizens. The question did not define what was meant by the term 'better citizens', and we should not assume that there is any commonly agreed definition of this term in a divided society. Nevertheless, the answers fell into what should now be an increasingly familiar pattern. Across all respondents, 57% agreed with this proposition. In general, then, people take the view that lifelong learning does make for better citizens, but this view was not nearly as widely shared as was the broadly favourable general attitude of the population at large towards lifelong learning in general. Once again, though, the responses fell into a marked bipolar pattern.

As Tables 3.5-3.8 show, the view that lifelong learning promotes better citizenship was much more widely held among those who thought it important to participate in each of the four civic activities examined.

Table 3.5: Percentage agreeing with statement: "Continuing to learn throughout life makes people better citizens"

Importance of own participation in community activities (OWN LEIS2)	Strongly agree /agree
Important	66.7
Neither	45.2
Not important	54.4

Table 3.6: Percentage agreeing with statement: "Continuing to learn throughout life makes people better citizens"

Importance of own participation in cultural events (OWN LEIS3)	Strongly agree/agree
Important	68.9
Neither	36.6
Not important	56.2

Table 3.7: Percentage agreeing with statement: "Continuing to learn throughout life makes people better citizens"

Importance of own participation in church activities (OWN LEIS4)	Strongly agree/agree
Important	61.8
Neither	41.1
Not important	56.6

Table 3.8: Percentage agreeing with statement: "Continuing to learn throughout life makes people better citizens"

Importance of own participation in sports (OWN LEIS1)	Strongly agree/agree
Important	60.9
Neither	50.7
Not important	55.8

These tables similarly confirm the bipolar distribution of responses, with a clear majority also agreeing with this view among those who counted the specific activities as unimportant. Those who held no particular view on the importance of each activity were also least likely to associate lifelong learning with citizenship. The gap between the active and the undecided was widest in respect of attitudes towards cultural activities, and lowest in respect of attitudes towards sports.

Respondents were also asked whether they believed government should be spending more on lifelong learning (Tables 3.9-3.12). Once again, the now familiar bipolar pattern appears for people involved in each of the four activities, with the gap between active and indifferent groups being

Table 3.9: Percentage agreeing with statement: "The government should be spending much more on providing lifelong learning for everyone"

Importance of own participation in community activities (OWN LEIS2)	Strongly agree/agree
Important	93.8
Neither	77.2
Not important	83.5

Table 3.10: Percentage agreeing with statement: "The government should be spending much more on providing lifelong learning for everyone"

Importance of own participation in cultural events (OWN LEIS3)	Strongly agree/agree
Important	94.4
Neither	77.0
Not important	83.7

Table 3.11: Percentage agreeing with statement: "The government should be spending much more on providing lifelong learning for everyone"

Importance of own participation in church activities (OWN LEIS4)	Strongly agree/agree
Important	90.1
Neither	67.7
Not important	86.5

Table 3.12: Percentage agreeing with statement: "The government should be spending much more on providing lifelong learning for everyone"

Importance of own participation in sports (OWN LEIS1)	Strongly agree/agree
Important	90.6
Neither	75.3
Not important	84.1

largest for people taking part in church activities. In each case, the most engaged are also those who show the highest levels of support for increased spending, followed by the unengaged; the undecided show the lowest levels of support.

Finally, NILTS allows us to consider the relationship between social capital and attitudes towards learning new technologies. The statement "It's impossible for people to keep up with all the new technology around at work these days" was included in NILTS as a way of exploring whether people felt overwhelmed by technological change (Tables 3.13-3.16). While not directly indicating a sense of fatalism or powerlessness, answers to this question might be taken as having some bearing on the extent to which people feel able to take charge of their own destinies.

Table 3.13: Percentage agreeing with statement: "It's impossible for people to keep up with all the new technology around at work these days"

Importance of own participation in community activities (OWN LEIS2)	Strongly agree/agree
Important	52.9
Neither	54.8
Not important	58.6

Table 3.14: Percentage agreeing with statement: "It's impossible for people to keep up with all the new technology around at work these days"

Importance of own participation in cultural events (OWN LEIS3)	Strongly agree/agree
Important	52.6
Neither	57.4
Not important	58.3

Table 3.15: Percentage agreeing with statement: "It's impossible for people to keep up with all the new technology around at work these days"

Importance of own participation in church activities (OWN LEIS4)	Strongly agree/agree
Important	56.2
Neither	60.4
Not important	55.8

Table 3.16: Percentage agreeing with statement: "It's impossible for people to keep up with all the new technology around at work these days"

Importance of own participation in sports (OWN LEIS1)	Strongly agree/agree
Important	53.6
Neither	45.2
Not important	59.8

Overall, 57% of the respondents agreed that it was impossible to keep up with new technology. Those who saw civic engagement as important were slightly less likely to take this view, with the exception of people involved in church activities who more or less reflected the general balance of opinion. With the exception of the church group, then, this is broadly consistent with the hypothesis that those with the most social capital are most likely to feel in charge of their lives. However, this needs to be qualified in two ways. First, differences between those who are more engaged and those who are less so are not very marked. In few cases is the gap larger than a handful of percentage points. It would therefore be wrong to read too much into such relatively insignificant differences. Second, the bipolar effect found in previous responses does not hold good across all the groups. In three of the four areas of civic engagement, those who view the activity as unimportant are also more likely to say that it is impossible to keep up with new technology. With the notable exception of sports activities, those who do not see civic activities as mattering one way or another come somewhere between the other two groups.

Of course, it is rather difficult to interpret answers to this question. The intention was primarily to discover whether respondents felt overwhelmed by technological change, or alternatively felt a degree of power to master it, but it is possible that some of those who said it was impossible to keep up with new technologies did so for other reasons (such as familiarity) while others who said they could do so were simply being unrealistic (based on poor knowledge). The responses of church members may reflect their average age, which tends to be higher than for other activities.

Yet, even given these qualifications, NILTS nonetheless is broadly consistent with the hypothesis that, with important exceptions, those who are active in civic activities are more likely to be confident about the possibilities of mastering the new technologies, and that those who are not active are less confident about this prospect. It would be stretching the data too far to suggest that this implies a general degree of empowerment as a result of engagement in voluntary activities. However, in this one area it seems that grappling with new knowledge and skills may be slightly less intimidating for the most socially connected than it is for the less engaged citizen. But the degree of variation in responses on this topic was relatively weak, and too much should not be read into this set of findings.

A further question concerned the extent to which workers might share responsibility for keeping their skills up to date (Tables 3.17-3.20). The question was posed in such a way as to leave entirely open the issue of who was paying for the learning, and to focus instead on the taking of responsibility for the learning itself. Once more the results show a clear

Table 3.17: Percentage agreeing with statement: "If the Northern Ireland economy is to be successful, workers will have to take responsibility for learning the skills that keep them up to date"

Importance of own participation in community activities (OWN LEIS2)	Strongly agree/agree
Important	86.8
Neither	78.4
Not important	79.5

Table 3.18: Percentage agreeing with statement: "If the Northern Ireland economy is to be successful, workers will have to take responsibility for learning the skills that keep them up to date"

Importance of own participation in cultural events (OWN LEIS3)	Strongly agree/agree
Important	84.8
Neither	72.1
Not important	82.9

Table 3.19: Percentage agreeing with statement: "If the Northern Ireland economy is to be successful, workers will have to take responsibility for learning the skills that keep them up to date"

Importance of own participation in church activities (OWN LEIS4)	Strongly agree/agree
Important	84.9
Neither	69.8
Not important	81.8

Table 3.20: Percentage agreeing with statement: "If the Northern Ireland economy is to be successful, workers will have to take responsibility for learning the skills that keep them up to date"

Importance of own participation in sports (OWN LEIS1)	Strongly agree/agree
Important	86.0
Neither	75.3
Not important	80.3

distribution. People who regarded a given associational activity as important or as unimportant were much more likely to say that workers should indeed take such responsibilities than people who said the activity was neither important nor unimportant in their own lives. This pattern was particularly marked in respect of church activities. Those who saw church as important and those who saw church as unimportant were almost equally likely to place some responsibility on the shoulders of workers; those who were indifferent or undecided about church activities were less likely than any other group in the survey to believe that workers should take responsibility for learning.

So far, then, the findings from NILTS indicate that levels of social capital and attitudes towards lifelong learning appear to be positively related. They also seem to suggest that people who are clearly not engaged in associational activities tend to be somewhat more favourable towards lifelong learning than people who are indifferent towards these activities. From an adult education providers' perspective, it might be said that people who actively dislike a given activity are more favourably disposed than are people who don't care much either way!

However, this pattern breaks down somewhat when we come to consider the extent of people's actual involvement in different types of organisations (Table 3.21). Once more, it seems that those who take some active part in the life of a given organisation are more favourably disposed towards lifelong learning than are either those who belong but have never taken an active part, or those who simply do not belong to that type of organisation (and both of the last two categories, of course, cover people who are members of, and possibly active in, other types of organisation than that named, along with those who belong to no group or organisation). So, once more we see evidence of joiners sharing more positive attitudes towards learning than non-joiners.

We also learn from the findings in Table 3.21 that organisations differ considerably in the extent to which their active members are favourably disposed towards learning. Those whose attitudes to learning are notably more positive than average include:

- those who belong to a union or professional association, whether active or not;
- those who belong to and have taken part in a church, a sports/hobby group, or a charitably body; and

Table 3.21: Percentage saying: "Learning in later life opens up a whole new world for people", by level of participation in groups and associations

	Have taken part	Belong but never taken part	Do not belong
Political party or club or association	80	85	86
Trades union or professional association	90	92	84
Church or other religious organisation	88	83	84
Sports group, hobby or leisure club	89	85	84
Charitable organisation or group	89	82	85
Neighbourhood association or group	86	83	85
Other association or group	80	94	86
All respondents	86		

- those who belong to but do not take part in groups in the 'other' category.

Beyond this, the only result which is relatively straightforward is that people who say they do not belong to a particular type of group are at the average or below it with respect to positive views on lifelong learning. Rather more complicated is the finding in respect of political parties and associations, where active members appear to be less positive towards learning than inactive members or non-members. This is a unique configuration of responses, but it may well reflect the rather fixed mindsets for which Northern Ireland's public political figures are famous ("open mouths and empty minds", as the saying has it). Given government policy on local area partnerships as a means of engaging the excluded, it is also worth noting that there is no particularly positive association between membership of neighbourhood groups and attitudes towards lifelong learning.

Finally, Table 3.22 presents a detailed breakdown of the 'joiners' responses to the three questions that were intended to point to broader value orientations. The three questions can in turn be seen as broad expressions of particular value orientations: (a) instrumentalism, (b) civic engagement

Table 3.22: Percentage of active members agreeing with opinion statements on lifelong learning among those who are active in groups and associations

	Instrumentalism: "Learning in later life is only worth doing if it will lead to something useful like a job or a promotion"	Civic engagement: "Continuing to learn throughout life makes people better citizens"	Resignation: It's impossible for people to keep up with all the new technology around at work these days"
Political party or club or association	39	49	58
Trades union or professional association	22	63	48
Church or other religious organisation	32	61	58
Sports group, hobby or leisure club	30	56	51
Charitable organisation or group	23	57	53
Neighbourhood association or group	33	51	53
Other association or group	23	49	45
All respondents	36	57	57

and (c) resignation. The findings once more suggest that different types of organisation are associated with different outlooks on learning.

Active members of political parties in Northern Ireland are more likely to hold an instrumental view of learning than average, and – perhaps ironically – are less likely to see learning as associated with civic engagement; they are as likely as the rest of the population to take a resigned or fatalistic view of the challenges involved in keeping abreast of new technologies. Active members of church groups, sports/hobby groups and neighbourhood groups are slightly less likely to adopt instrumental views of learning, slightly more inclined towards a belief in civic outcomes (again, though, neighbourhood groups are a notable exception to this), and slightly less resigned to the impossibility of dealing with new technology (with church members constituting an exception on this count). Active members of trades unions, charitable groups and 'other' bodies are much less likely to take an instrumental view of learning, and are generally less resigned in the face of technological change; with the exception of those involved in charities, they are also more inclined to associate learning with civic outcomes. The slightly maverick pattern shown for those involved in charities may reflect the close links between the main churches and some of the more significant charities.

Members of unions and professional associations stand out as being the least instrumental group and also the most civically minded, as well as the least fatalistic. So, once more, the message appears to be that social capital should not be viewed in a simplistic way. While joining makes a difference, what is more important is probably the type of organisation that is being joined, with some being much more conservative than others in their approach to learning and change in later life.

In general, then, it is possible to conclude that the NILTS findings do indeed show a very distinctive pattern. Those who see civic engagement as important in their own lives are, by and large, the most likely to value lifelong learning as a force for personal emancipation; they are also the most likely to see it as helping to foster active citizenship, and the most likely to favour increased public spending on it; they are the least likely to feel overwhelmed by the new technologies.

So far, this is consistent with the existing literature on active citizenship and adult learning. What is new is the finding that the disengaged are in fact divided, with those who believe that a civic activity is not important in their lives showing much more positive attitudes towards lifelong learning than those who are undecided. This group also falls in between the active and the undecided in respect of government spending and the impact of adult learning on active citizenship, and generally occupies the same place with respect to its attitude towards technological change.

This is an important finding, suggesting that any simplistic distinction between the 'engaged' and the 'disengaged' is somewhat misleading. Also, in general, it has to be said that while there are marked differences between the more and the least engaged, these are differences of degree. There are no grounds for deducing that there is a simple equation between engagement and learning, such that those who are most engaged all demonstrate favourable attitudes while the least engaged all demonstrate unfavourable ones. The survey data depict a broad positive association between engagement and learning, but the bald statistics should not lead us to underestimate the ambiguity of these findings.

Lessons from the quantitative data

Putnam's definition of social capital is largely couched in terms of civic engagement plus shared norms and trust. Like most other researchers, he uses the term to encompass a wider range of phenomena than those usually referred to as active citizenship. In his work on Italy (1993), for example, he highlighted the contribution of choirs and, in his studies of community in the US (1995, 2000), he has shown considerable interest in what is happening in the world of bowling. The evidence presented in his 1995 paper on the US takes a similarly broad view of social capital, encompassing involvement in church activities, cultural activities and sports alongside involvement in community-based and voluntary organisations.

In summary, the Northern Ireland survey data confirm other studies – including the 2002 omnibus adult learning survey – that have found a link between social capital and lifelong learning. More specifically, this study demonstrates a positive association between attitudes towards civic engagement and adult learning. Of course, it would be wrong to read too much into the findings of one survey, such as NILTS; moreover, like any survey, it can tell us little about patterns of causation. What it does provide is clear evidence of a positive attitudinal association in one particular context, at one particular time. However, as we have seen, the link between learning and engagement was also found in the 2002 adult learning survey. This is broadly consistent with Szreter's account of networks as channels for sharing information and encouraging adoption of new ideas and techniques (Szreter, 2000).

Both surveys also seem to show that engagement is not a simple and undifferentiated process, at least in terms of its association with learning. Some of the types of engagement here are clearly home-based and may be carried out by a solitary individual. Gardening is an example that springs to mind; and, while it is true that gardeners can swap seeds and cuttings, it is also true that collective forms of gardening, such as allotments, are in sharp decline. In the 2002 adult learning survey, regular gardeners showed relatively low levels of involvement in learning, while those who went out to socialise showed relatively high levels. If the degree of solitariness and gregariousness inherent in the activity provides one set of poles, another set is constituted by the type of organisation. Those that bring together people around a single set of values, such as a church, tend to be associated with very different attitudes from those who bring together people with divergent values, such as unions and professional associations. This appears to confirm the significance of heterogeneity (Morgan, 2000) in associations. However, both types of involvement were broadly associated in NILTS with positive views on learning, so the key message here is that some engagement appears – all other things being equal – to be better than none.

The findings also suggest that it is wrong to think of disengagement as a clear-cut and undifferentiated form of behaviour. In NILTS, the least well disposed towards lifelong learning were those who were uncertain or indifferent towards particular forms of civic engagement. Those who were definite about their non-involvement came somewhere in the middle in respect of their attitudes towards lifelong learning: while they tended to be less enthusiastic than the activists, they were much more positive than the indifferent. This is consistent with research by political scientists into the causes of electoral apathy, which has shown that non-voters stay away during elections for a variety of reasons. In the recent elections for the Scottish Parliament, for example, 31% of non-voters made the decision to stay away over a month before the poll; many non-voters were found by the researchers to offer 'good reasons' for not turning out (Boon and Curtice, 2003, p 19). Similarly, the attitudes of NILTS respondents clearly differ to a marked extent depending on the nature of their non-engagement.

Finally, it has to be said that, although there is a clear statistical relationship between social capital and adult learning, on the evidence considered in this chapter it is not a particularly strong one. There are clear distinctions between the responses of those who are engaged in a given activity and those who are not, but in no case is the gap a massive one. We are therefore talking about differences of degree, of shading and overlap, rather than a black and white division. What this suggests is that the particular attitudes expressed by respondents may well be contingent, and therefore open to change.

Despite these qualifications, the survey data show that there are broad attitudinal clusters that appear to hang together. This in turn suggests the possibility of wider sets of dispositions, which are also connected to people's educational trajectories and socioeconomic situation. This is, it should be emphasised, somewhat speculative. Crudely, though, it appears possible to distinguish very tentatively between three broad groups or clusters. These might be very roughly described as follows:

- "Not me pal". Around 15% of the population are sceptical about lifelong learning's capacity for promoting change. People in this group are also the least likely to be engaged in civic activity, but are not actively rejecting it. In socioeconomic terms they are relatively disadvantaged, coming from the old manual worker milieu or the ranks of the long-term unemployed; their educational trajectories were generally completed by the time they left school. Although this chapter has not considered evidence on bonding social capital, in the form of close kinship and neighbourhood ties, it seems likely that this type of social capital is characteristic of this group. This group is most likely to find itself engaging in those types of formal instruction that are targeted at those who are most at risk of social exclusion.
- "It all depends". This group accepts that lifelong learning can foster change and development. Its members have a clear view of the importance of specific activities; either they are involved or they are not. In some cases, they explicitly reject a particular form of engagement (such as church activity), rather than affecting indecision or indifference. They tend to be relatively well educated, often including periods of post-school education, and come from the manual working class and the middle class alike. The group's social capital is likely to reflect a mixture of bonding and bridging ties. In approaching formal learning, people may adopt a somewhat defensive rather than active orientation, but they are nonetheless willing to participate if they can see something concrete as a potentially achievable result.
- "Learning is my way of life". This group actively embraces lifelong learning, as a means of both personal growth and communal capacity building. It is the most likely to place importance on civic activity as an element in one's own life. Again, it is relatively well educated, including significant phases of post-school education, and comes from both the rising working class and the middle class (particularly the service professionals). While it may be able to access bonding ties, it is likely also to have access to bridging and some linking ties.

Considerably further work would be required to refine this somewhat speculative and undeveloped analysis, possibly along the lines of the social milieu analysis pioneered by Michael Vester and his colleagues in Germany (Vester, 1997). What we can say is that, although there is substantial evidence to confirm the existence of a generally positive relationship between social capital and lifelong learning, it appears to be multiplex and multidirectional, rather than being linear and monocausal. While the idea of a linkage may well appeal to policy makers and professional educationalists, then, it must be seen as a highly complex one, in which poorly designed interventions carry a high risk of unintended consequences.

Yet, despite the complexities, the central message of this chapter is that civic engagement and active learning are both bound up with a sense of agency. By this, I mean first that people are in a position where they feel that, to some extent at least, they are agents of their own fate; and, second, not only do they feel themselves to be able to exercise some control over their destiny, they are also able to develop and use their capabilities for action in the wider world – economically, socially and politically. This is not, of course, in itself a judgement on the structure of opportunities that may offer or deny opportunities to use these capabilities. Yet, as Amartya Sen has argued, governments are far more likely to impose supposedly 'ideal' solutions on populations that they deem to be passive, while people's capabilities for exercising their freedoms are much more likely to further democracy and development (Sen, 1999). These are large and ambitious goals, but they also possess intimate and everyday implications. Lifelong learning and civic engagement are important sources of agency, both in themselves and in the capabilities that they help people to realise.

Note

[1] Further details on the questionnaire design, survey method and findings of NILTS can be found on the website (www.ark.ac.uk/nilt). My own involvement with NILTS, 2001, was as adviser to the module on lifelong learning, where I was involved in questionnaire design and analysis of the findings. The questionnaires themselves were conducted by Research and Evaluation Services, and the survey was overseen by teams from the two Northern Ireland universities. I owe particular thanks to Anne-Marie Gray (University of Ulster) and Katrina Lloyd (Queen's University, Belfast) for their advice, guidance and patience.

FOUR

Rethinking the relationship

While much previous research has concentrated on schools, and has focused on parents rather than learners, this book studies the way that social capital and learning interact among adults. I have used a differentiated and relatively broad definition of social capital, encompassing engagement in voluntary associations, sports and leisure groups, and community bodies, as well as relationships arising from kinship and neighbourhood. This approach suggests that the relationship between people's networks and the learning they undertake is extremely complex, and is often very much bound up with particular contexts and even with specific life events.

Moreover, social capital and adult learning are sometimes linked in a virtuous cycle, but sometimes they can substitute for one another, and they can also cut across one another. In some circumstances, when it comes to new ideas or skills or information, many people prefer to trust their networks rather than rely on educational institutions. Nevertheless, the findings broadly confirm that at the most general level, and all other things being equal, people who have the most connections are the most positive about learning in adult life, and are more likely to participate in organised learning than people who are more isolated. They also indicate that networks consisting mainly of bonding ties – such as close family and neighbours – release a more limited and less heterodox range of information and knowledge than networks that contain a range of bridging and scaling ties. Finally, all attempts to analyse the interplay of networks and learning need to be set against a wider context, in which all material assets are very unequally distributed.

This chapter considers the extent to which these findings might influence the general ways we look at learning and social capital. Of course, if the nature of network resources is context-dependent, then we need to consider the specific nature of the area under study. The chapter therefore opens with a brief discussion of some of Northern Ireland's distinctive characteristics, with a view to establishing the limitations that these might impose on the wider relevance of this study. The next sections review the findings from recent research into the relationship between networks and learning. The chapter then goes on to examine the significance of this study for our understanding of social capital, taking into account some of the changes that are taking place in the way that people and communities relate to one another. It particularly argues the need for a differentiated rather than a univocal model of social capital when considering the implications for our understanding of learning, particularly in adult life.

The significance of context

This book has sought to explore the influence that people's connections have on their access to skills, knowledge and ideas. The evidence presented here was collected in Northern Ireland, and it would be foolhardy to assume that similar patterns prevail everywhere. Particularly relevant for this study, perhaps, is the fact that it is relatively small and compact: the 2001 Census recorded a population of 1,685,267, and under one in a hundred came from a minority ethnic community (NISRA, 2002, p 18). Yet Northern Ireland also shares a large number of common features with other western societies, above all perhaps that I undertook the research in the context of a society that by global standards is affluent, highly educated and safe.

Compared with the rest of northern Europe, Northern Ireland has a reputation for violence and danger. Without in any way minimising the misery caused by the Troubles, a glance at official statistics will tell us that levels of recorded violence are not especially high (and my experience, like that of many others, is that public interpersonal encounters almost invariably feel warm and open). Its social arrangements might appear somewhat traditional, centred as they are on family and close friends; the churches are probably stronger than in most of northern Europe, so that faith-based social capital is relatively dense. More widely, given the nature of the ethno-religious division within Northern Ireland, we could see much networking – and the resources thereby made accessible – as being generated within each community at least in part by opposition to the social capital of members of the other faith, and tending to favour bonding ties as safer than ties with people who are not already well known. So, social capital is borne at least partly out of defensive responses to perceived threats (not simply or even mainly physical) from the other community; it is relatively dense, with central nodes around kinship and faith. Bonding social capital is strong, then, but there are also abundant stocks of what Woolcock defines as linking social capital, spanning socioeconomic, spatial and gender-based divides (Woolcock, 1998).

In most other respects, though, I think of Northern Ireland as much like the rest of western and northern Europe, but friendlier and with a more temperate climate. This rather limits the relevance of this study for non-western societies, a constraint that needs to be emphasised given the considerable interest shown in recent years in applying the concept of social capital to economic development in the developing nations, where the World Bank has proven a particularly influential voice (see the relevant section of the World Bank website [www.worldbank.org/poverty/scapital/]). Its households on average are slightly poorer than in the Irish Republic or Britain, and socioeconomic inequalities – which exist elsewhere, of course – are deeply marked by a legacy of discrimination and coercion. But, by global standards, it is a rich place. Its economy has followed a similar pattern to that of other western European nations, with a marked shift since the 1970s away from manufacturing and extraction, and a dramatic growth in service industries. It is also affected by the same general sociocultural and economic trends as the rest of western society.

In addition, this study is based on evidence collected at the turn of the millennium, drawing on data gathered between 1998 and 2002. Social scientists sometimes present their analyses as timeless, as though only the specificities of place are important. History also counts, and many people think that it matters, particularly in Northern Ireland. This study took place while the peace process was very fragile, and the cease-fires were constantly at risk of breaking down; this took place against a backdrop of continuing sectarian tension during the summer parading season, as well as constant and persistent violence around the fringes of paramilitarism. Uncertainty was accompanied by a sense of excitement at the possibilities. "We've got our own city back", one Belfast interviewee told me in the car park after a focus group.

The Northern Ireland that followed the hopes and uncertainties of the millennium seemed in some ways a more settled society, with rapid economic growth in the main urban areas, a sharp increase and diversification in consumer and leisure services in Belfast and Derry, and an enormous rise in travel and freight traffic with neighbouring countries. Yet this emerging culture of prosperity and consumer choice was accompanied by symptoms of collapse in established social support systems; to take only two rather distressing examples, youth suicide rates were rising, and partially demobilised paramilitary movements started to engage in what had previously been known sardonically as 'ordinary decent crime'. Northern Ireland has a comparatively youthful population (NISRA, 2002, p 10), and we might expect that social norms and behaviour will continue to change rapidly in the new circumstances that are following the peace processes of the late 1990s. The conditions studied in this volume no longer exist.

Specificities of time and space matter. The approach taken in this book is one that treats culture and behaviour as material forces, constructed by living people in specific circumstances, and with access to unequally distributed assets. It has to be acknowledged at the outset that these specificities place obvious limitations on the wider relevance of this study, but these must be placed in perspective: in most respects, Northern Ireland at the turn of the millennium was also recognisably one of the many varied regions of contemporary western Europe. This being so, we can be reasonably confident that some of the relationships between networks and learning can be found in other comparable societies. This is confirmed by two recent empirical studies, drawing on rather different sets of evidence, of the relations between social capital and adult learning. However, even this is to miss the point: as Bourdieu insisted, social practices are always inherently spatial in character (see Savage et al, 2005, pp 97-101), and I would add that they are also bound by and constructed over time. In this sense, the general representativeness of this or that locale is beside the point. People's social relationships and cultural norms form part of a specific habitus, which is constituted through and in particular places and times.

Social capital influences learning

Much of this book has argued that people's networks have an influence on their learning. The evidence presented thus far suggests that the relationship between human capital and social capital is a complex one. The qualitative evidence in Chapter Two showed that, in Northern Ireland, social network resources can provide people with a very effective substitute for human capital. The quantitative evidence in Chapter Three confirmed that there is a tendency for attitudes towards learning to be positively associated with levels of civic engagement, but this was a tendency rather than an absolute correlation. In short, judging by the quantitative evidence, the relationship was, while clear, not particularly strong. In order to make sense of the influence of social capital on learning, it was suggested at the end of Chapter Three that we need to know far more about people's general dispositions, and about their objective socioeconomic position.

This is some way from James Coleman's straightforward description of social capital and human capital forming a virtuous circle, with each mutually reinforcing the other in a relatively linear manner (Coleman, 1988-89). Of course, it should be said at the outset that Coleman's interest lay in the education of children, while the present study is of course concerned mainly with learning in adult life. Moreover, his definition of social capital gives primacy to close kinship ties, in particular those based on birth, and to ties associated with membership of a particular faith community. It has already been shown that people in Northern Ireland share both high levels of social capital resources of both types, but the present study also looked at broader patterns of civic engagement as well as family ties and church activities.

Among the adults in this study, a virtuous circle appeared to hold good at a very general level, in so far as people who are engaged in civic activities tend also to take a positive view of learning. Yet this association was a relatively weak one. There was also some evidence in the 2002 adult learning survey to indicate that people whose leisure interests are largely home-based are less likely to be involved in learning than are people whose leisure interests take them out of the home. Moreover, the qualitative evidence suggested that close family ties and neighbourhood ties might serve as a substitute for participation in formal learning. The survey evidence also showed that different types of civic engagement were associated with different sets of attitudes towards learning. Overall, this study has also shown that high levels of social capital resources in Northern Ireland do indeed seem to be associated with strong achievement in schools, but they are also associated with comparatively low levels of participation in almost all forms of organised adult learning. Given the importance of participation in the adult education literature, this finding merits further discussion.

The most significant study elsewhere of the impact of social capital on adult learning is Clare Strawn's study of longitudinal survey data for Portland, Oregon (Strawn, 2002, 2003). This study was designed to explore the impact of social capital, socioeconomic position and 'discourse community' (in other words, the language people use in their personal communities to describe attitudes towards learning) on participation in either formal or informal learning. Informal learning was operationalised in terms of reading plus at least one other self-directed activity, such as asking someone; Strawn's data came from the Longitudinal Study of Adult Learning (LSAL), which interviewed 940 adults who had not completed high school or obtained the high school diploma; half the sample had attended at least one adult basic education (ABE) or a preparation class for the high school diploma, and the other half was drawn at random from the local population. As well as the interview, participants also completed standardised literacy assignments (Strawn, 2003, pp 29-30).

Strawn's analysis showed that the impact of social capital varied considerably for different types of network, and it varied as between formal and informal learning. People with strong and tight networks, and those whose networks were based around their family, were both less likely than others to participate in formal adult learning programmes (Strawn, 2003, p 42). People with large networks were rather more likely to participate in formal programmes, and there was a small association between participation and generalised trust (Strawn, 2003, p 43). On the whole, then, social capital tended to predict low participation in formal learning.

Informal learning, on the other hand, is greatly facilitated by the range and closeness of people's connections. Strawn showed that any form of network was associated with informal learning; in particular, people with mainly family-based ties were almost five times as likely than relatively isolated people to engage in informal learning but, in general, close networks were found to predict participation, while civic engagement tended to predict non-participation (Strawn, 2003, p 45; see also the similar pattern for civic engagement reported in Dakhli and de Clercq, 2004, p 119). Membership of a 'discourse community' that expressed favourable attitudes towards education appeared only to increase participation among people with particularly dense networks; otherwise, the shared norms of peers appeared to have a rather limited impact (Strawn, 2003, p 48). People who reported no civic activities at all, and those who reported more than one, were both more likely to engage in informal learning than people reporting only one civic activity (Strawn, 2003, p 54).

Strawn's conclusion was that social capital influenced learning "in opposite directions: positively for informal learning and negatively for formal learning" (Strawn, 2003, p 51). These findings are partly compatible with the evidence from the Northern Ireland studies. Respondents in Portland with dense and family-based ties showed a marked preference for informal learning through personal and community support networks, and this is broadly consistent with the use of informal learning mechanisms found in Northern Ireland. There is also some evidence in Strawn's study, albeit limited, that those with no civic activities and those with several are more likely to participate than those with only one activity (usually voting). Again, this is reminiscent of the bipolar pattern found in responses to the Northern Ireland Life and Times Survey (NILTS). Yet Strawn's data do not confirm the broadly positive attitude towards lifelong learning that was found among the most engaged in Northern Ireland. Interestingly, the most positive attitudes in the Portland study were found among respondents whose networks Strawn characterised as open, and the least positive among those with large networks (Strawn, 2003, p 50). So this part of Strawn's study points in a slightly different direction from the Northern Ireland findings.

However, we should first note some of the limitations associated with the Portland study. First, it was designed specifically to examine relations between networks and learning among a clearly defined and limited population – namely, people with relatively low levels of formal educational attainment. Yet participation in adult learning and civic activities are both closely correlated with educational attainment and socioeconomic status (Field, 2003a). Strawn's work is particularly significant precisely because she draws a picture of learning and networks among those at the lower end of the socioeconomic scale, but this does also place a clear limitation on the scope of her study. Further, her study used statistical methods to analyse longitudinal data. This is a considerable strength in that she is able to suggest patterns of causality rather more clearly than I was able to on the basis of NILTS. However, the absence of qualitative data means that issues of meaning and understanding cannot be explored in any depth. Finally, the LSAL questionnaire defined formal learning in a rather limited way (Strawn, 2003, p 73); while this has the benefit of clarity and precision, it does mean that other types of learning are excluded. These comments are intended not as criticisms of what remains a landmark study; rather, they point to some of the limitations that were built into its design.

Strawn's work provides an important foundation for future studies by providing clear evidence of the substitutability of social capital and human capital, and further undermining the simplistic models that can be derived from Coleman and Putnam. While there are differences between her findings and those presented in Chapters Two and Three of this book, some of these arise from the different research methods used, which allow her to go further in some respects and limit her work in others, while others are relatively trivial. Given the differences of context between Portland and Northern Ireland, the real surprise is that the findings are in agreement on some key issues, including the significance of networks for informal learning, and the possible downward influence of networks on aspirations and interests in formal learning. These are important findings by any account, particularly when set against the persistent evidence of complex but marked relationships between social capital and adult learning at a variety of different levels.

Learning influences social capital

Much existing research into adult learning is concerned with explaining patterns of participation and non-participation. Studies of the impact of adult learning are less common. As Tom Schuller has pointed out, "the ways in which learning actually affects our lives, individually and collectively, remain relatively unexplored in systematic empirical fashion" (Schuller, 2004a, p 3). Anecdotal evidence is available in plenty but, as usual with such individual stories, one person's experience of liberation and fulfilment is always matched by another's narrative of boredom and waste. Those studies that exist of the impact of learning have largely tended to focus either on the educational outcomes of learning (defined in terms of qualifications and progression to other learning activities) or on the economic outcomes (usually expressed in terms of changes in earnings, and more rarely in terms of the broad impact on the economy). Until recently, the non-economic and non-educational consequences of people's learning remained a largely unexplored area.

This gap is, though, steadily being plugged. The Research Centre on the Wider Benefits of Learning (WBL), created in 1999 at the University of London, has conducted a series of major studies of the ways in which adult learning can contribute to four broad areas: social cohesion, active citizenship, active aging and public health (Schuller et al, 2004). Drawing on interviews conducted in three different English districts, as well as on new analyses of existing quantitative datasets (primarily the 1958 and 1970 British Birth Cohort Studies), the WBL team examined the negative as well as the positive consequences of learning for the four areas. While the results of this study are of considerable general significance for our understanding of the part that learning plays in people's lives, the sections of particular interest for this book are the findings in respect of social cohesion and active citizenship.

The 1958 cohort study provides data on the participants' experiences and behaviour at a number of stages in their lives; the WBL team was concerned with adult life, and concentrated on the impact of formal learning undertaken between the ages of 33 and 42. Overall, the analysis found that the apparent effects of taking one or two courses at this stage of life included significant growth in levels of racial tolerance and in memberships of civic associations, as well as smaller but marked growth in levels of political interest and electoral participation, and some decline in political cynicism and authoritarianism (Bynner and Hammond, 2004, p 167). They also showed that, in general, the more courses taken, the more marked were these changes (Bynner and Hammond, 2004, p 170).

The WBL studies provide extremely important insights into the contribution of learning to social capital. Of course, we cannot be entirely certain what is cause and what is effect; nor is it yet clear just how this relationship works. But there are very significant clues in the WBL studies. The first comes in the contrasting experiences of people on vocational and academic courses. Interestingly, the study found that these changes were largely the result of participation in academic courses, where the quantitative analysis showed that the consequences were found among people who were relatively isolated and lacking in confidence when their courses began, and among those who took non-accredited courses, whereas the interview subjects were likely to have been fairly active and tolerant already. Very few social capital benefits arose from participation between the ages of 33 and 42 in vocational courses – which, ironically, also brought people no identifiable economic benefits (Bynner and Hammond, 2004, p 176). An obvious explanation of this difference lies in the agency of the individuals who undertook the learning. Adults aged between 33 and 42 are only likely to take an academic course if they choose to do so, particularly if it does not lead to a qualification. By contrast, people taking vocational courses are often motivated by external factors, such as a change in regulatory frameworks or a desire to pass an exam that might lead to promotion; they may well be on the course because someone else – an employer, a welfare agency, a magistrate – has told them to attend (the somewhat neglected topic of compulsion in lifelong learning is discussed further in Field, 2000, pp 118-24). There may also be question marks over the quality of some vocational provision, which in certain cases can be superficial or even – in some cases – non-existent (Field, 2000, p 28; Bynner and Hammond, 2004, p 177).

A second pointer can be found in evidence that learning can provide people with capabilities that promote engagement with others. Political scientists rightly point to the way in which civic activity is shaped by political structures, and particularly by the opportunities that these offer to citizens not only to join in but also to exercise significant and visible influence over events (Maloney et al, 2000a, 2000b). Wider social and economic inequalities also impose powerful constraints on some people. Nevertheless, the WBL studies also provide evidence – qualitative and statistical – of the impact of learning on what we might call social meta-competences, such as confidence and self-efficacy, including either turning around or reinforcing the low self-esteem caused by poor schooling (Hammond, 2004, pp 42-5). In other words, learning appears to affect not simply someone's decision whether or not to participate, it also gives them access to information concerning the opportunities and likely results of participation, and equips them with specific sets of skills and understanding associated with citizenship. Learning also boosts – or, if the experience is a poor one, undermines – the underlying capabilities required in order to participate and improve the likelihood of positive outcomes from participation.

So, there is now a growing, and I would argue increasingly convincing, body of evidence on the relations between social capital and adult learning. Taken together, Strawn's findings and the material presented in earlier chapters here suggest not only that people's networks and engagement play an important role in shaping attitudes towards and participation in learning defined as formal education and training, but that they also provide powerful and effective opportunities for informal learning, and may therefore create substitutes for more conventional forms of human capital investment. The WBL studies show that learning also shapes people's access to social capital resources, and provides significant indications of how this influence occurs. Of course, much remains to be done. As Strawn says, this area of research is still "a rich field of enquiry" (Strawn, 2003, p 64).

But, at the very least, we should now be in a position to acknowledge the importance of the relationship. The legitimacy of this area of research is no longer in question: social capital is important for learning, and learning is important for social capital. But, just as we reach these conclusions, we are forced to acknowledge that they must be provisional, resting as they do on studies of phenomena – learning and networks – that are very broad, hard to measure and constantly changing. The very idea of social capital, it is said, "perhaps matches the spirit of an uncertain, questing age" (Schuller et al, 2000, p 92). According to the most celebrated scholar of social capital, people's stocks of community are dwindling rapidly, and societies are thereby losing access to the resources that allow them to cooperate effectively for mutual purposes (Putnam, 1995, 2000). So, perhaps, just as we come to recognise the ways in which social capital and learning interact, we are studying something that will shortly belong to the past rather than the future.

The changing shape of community in western societies

Robert Putnam has famously used the metaphor of bowling to draw attention to his argument. Whereas Americans used to bowl in leagues, where one team competed against another, now they 'bowl alone'. While this graphic image captures our attention, Putnam follows it up with a thorough, detailed and systematic analysis of organisations' membership records, social attitudes survey data and other studies of public behaviour to demonstrate that Americans are meeting up with fewer people, and are doing so on a more and more irregular basis. Rather than spending time with others, they increasingly staying at home engaging in isolated and passive electronic entertainments, taking time out occasionally to drive from their suburban homes to anonymous malls (Putnam, 2000). Does this mean, Putnam goes on to claim, that stocks of social capital are diminishing in western societies?

My own answer to this question is that social capital is alive and well, but it is undoubtedly changing (Field, 2003a, pp 93-101). Putnam's data are compelling, but they come mainly from organisations whose heyday is over. It is as though we drew a picture of British civic society based on evidence of decline in the Women's Institutes, non-conformist chapels, trades unions and branches of the Conservative and Labour parties. While all of these organisations remain powerful influences in contemporary Britain (with the exception of the chapels), their membership levels have plummeted, and members are usually elderly; very few people turn up to meetings or take part in their other internal or public activities. But is it simply that we are increasingly disengaged from public life, and sit around the house gazing listlessly at a shimmering screen? Or is something else going on in our lives, which is perhaps slightly more complex than Putnam thinks?

My own perspective on these issues is influenced in large part by a group of contemporary sociologists who have been described – by others, not themselves – as espousing 'reflexive modernisation theory'. As well as Anthony Giddens and Barbara Misztal, this grouping includes the prominent German social theorist, Ulrich Beck, who has argued that western societies are becoming increasingly individualised, in the sense that people's life courses and consequent bodies of experience are increasingly differentiated, and that people also prize autonomy and choice as key life objects (Beck, 2000). Giddens' idea of self-identity in late modernity (1991) as well as Beck's hypothesis of the 'risk society' both point to ways in which people continually review their affiliations, taking a reflexive and questioning approach to social institutions of all kinds – including all those grouped together under the banner of social capital.

Beck, Giddens and Misztal share a belief that this process is happening at least partly because people are increasingly able to draw on a range of information and ideas that provide them with choices – or even confront them with the need for choices – which require reflection on the options available. Yet, each option is twinned with a variety of alternative options, and the information available points in a variety of different directions. A number of commentators have noted that this account is also a way of presenting a narrative of a learning society (Field, 2000, pp 59-63; Schemmann, 2002), in which people bring resources of different kinds to bear upon their knowledge capabilities. Also, of course, it is consistent with the general approach of this book that one of those reasons will include people's access to social capital resources. At the same time, there are also bound to be implications for the nature of people's social networks. Taking the most obvious tack, it might reasonably be thought that a general trend towards individualisation is likely to erode people's stocks of social capital. Is there anything in this and, if so, what are the implications for adult learning?

As we have seen, Putnam's answer is forthright: stocks of social capital are in freefall. Even informal sociability is, he believes, less frequent and widespread than it used to be; antisocial behaviour, by contrast, is on the rise (Putnam, 2000). Nor is Putnam alone in lamenting a collapse in community and family since the Second World War (Etzioni, 1995). Yet change is not always the same as loss. Social life is constantly changing, and it would be surprising if the patterns of people's networks remained static and fixed. Four examples can be taken, all of which are selected because of their relevance to the connections between networks and learning: the family, active citizenship, work and the new technologies. No doubt many other examples could have been considered, but these are enough to provide some detail to support the general pointers.

The first area is that of intimate relationships, including the family. It is quite obvious that the family is undergoing a process of transformation. People's close intimate relationships no longer fit the simplistic pattern of the patriarchal family that in the 1950s appeared to represent normality. Sexual partnerships, childrearing arrangements, support structures for older people, even the decisions whether to have children or offer support to the infirm – all these arrangements are increasingly diverse, and tend to be less bound by habit and more by choice than was the case 50 years ago. Also, while younger people have been faster to adopt the new arrangements, they are far from unknown among older people; even among those born well before 1945, unmarried partnerships (including live-apart relationships) are much more common than they were two or three decades ago (Dykstra, 2004). At the same time as older family relations are giving way to what Giddens has described as "pure relationships" – that is, relationships entered into and sustained for their own sake, rather than from deference to external sanctions such as those of the church (Giddens, 1992) – so trust and faithfulness become more important bases for family life. Yet, precisely for this reason, pure relationships are more vulnerable to disruption caused by breakdown of trust arising from the disclosure of unfaithful behaviour (Misztal, 1996, p 161). Conventional family life is, in these circumstances, as likely to destroy social capital and erode trust as build them. Divorced people provide a readership base for at least one specialist magazine, full of self-help coping tips for the newly single woman (Thorpe, 2000). Divorced men, by contrast, are more prone either to loneliness or to rapid remarriage.

Do these shifts herald the displacement of lasting heterosexual bonds, designed to provide a secure environment for rearing children, by more flexible, diverse and risky sets of arrangements? If so, are these part of a wider shift, away from unreflexive commitment and towards a more provisional and conditional form of intimacy? What might these trends mean for the socialisation of young people, as well as the capacity of adults to access and create new information and knowledge through their kinship bonds? Of course, it is possible to exaggerate the extent of these shifts. As Lynn Jamieson notes, most forms of cohabiting are basically very similar, and involve broadly comparable expectations between the partners in the relationship (Jamieson, 1998, p 33). New types of family, at least among heterosexual couples, have involved "relatively modest change in gender inequalities" within the home, and also among wider friendship networks (Jamieson, 1998, p 166). It would be going too far to claim that intimacy is giving way to 'thintimacy'.

Yet, however unevenly, there are at least marked tendencies towards more reflexive, conditional and provisional forms of intimacy. Whatever the benefits of these tendencies for those affected, Jamieson also notes that light-touch intimate partnerships do tend to carry high risks of breakdown, which can in turn disrupt wider networks of connections, both for kin (grandchildren/grandparents) and for friends. Not only are these then disruptive for the identity formation of children, if childrearing is involved, but "a pattern of fragile serial relationships of intense disclosing intimacy" can also subvert and damage the identity and self-confidence of the adult partners themselves (Jamieson, 1998, p 155). Much recent research on the new shape of family life has tended to confirm that Coleman's formulation of social capital does not correspond to the realities of contemporary kinship. Yet, if Coleman was wrong to see the growth of single-parent households and related trends as threatening the overall stocks of social capital (Seaman and Sweeting, 2004), the new trends have certainly affected the immediate contexts within which people's bonds are formed and understood. To the extent that such tendencies are touching the lives of adults, they are likely to have an influence on people's abilities to use their most immediate kin-based networks to access and create knowledge.

While family was central to Coleman's model of social capital, civic engagement is central to Putnam's diagnosis of community decline. Voluntary organisations and similar collective endeavours are, for Putnam, the central fields in which citizens develop a shared understanding and learn trust; without these, there is no wider reservoir of reciprocity for a society to draw upon. His evidence of decline in a wide range of membership organisations, from the Buffaloes to organised sport, from political bodies to trades unions, leads him to conclude that the principles and practices of reciprocity are under a powerful long-term threat. Putnam's evidence, though drawn from a very wide set of sources, is not comprehensive, and a number of commentators have suggested that American community is in better shape than he has claimed (Field, 2003a). Rather sharper arguments have been put forward in respect of western European societies, where it appears that civic engagement may be changing but is not necessarily declining (Hall, 1999). Where there is evidence of decline, moreover, it seems to be concentrated in certain areas.

An important, detailed analysis of long-term trends in Britain has concluded that the levels of social capital are indeed changing, but they are doing so unevenly (Li et al, 2003). Basically, a large fall in 'labour'-type participation (unions, working men's clubs, and so on) has been offset partially by a small but significant growth since the 1970s in other types of civic activities. Given the class biases of these patterns, middle-class participation appears to have remained stable, while working-class participation has fallen sharply; and this over a period when the middle class has grown markedly, while the working class has shrunk. The same study also shows a marked gender effect, with men being more likely to participate in formal civic associations than women; yet the marked class effect holds good for people of both genders and is much stronger than the differences between men and women, and it also looks as though the gap between men and women in similar social positions is shrinking over time. The authors conclude that: "It is those in working-class positions, poorly-educated and without service-class friends who are most likely to be disengaged from, hence deprived of access to, any formal channels of social capital. This is particularly true of women in these positions" (Li et al, 2003, p 519).

In terms of civic participation, then, Putnam may be right to point to a general decline. However, it appears to be much slower and more uneven than he suggests; and he appears to have missed altogether evidence of a marked socioeconomic polarisation in people's stocks of social capital.

For many people, social connections are closely bound up with place of work. Despite abundant evidence on the importance of work in people's everyday lives, workplace connections are a somewhat neglected area in the otherwise burgeoning literature on social capital. This might be considered surprising given the importance of work and workplaces in the literature on social networks, which have long been recognised as playing a significant role in jobseekers' behaviour (Granovetter, 1973), in people's occupational and class identities, and in respect of innovation and entrepreneurial success (Field, 2003a, pp 50-7). Work is also an important site of both formal and informal learning, so it is important to examine the ways in which its organisation and nature appear to be changing.

Factors such as technological change and globalisation are routinely cited as sources of economic change. Particularly in western societies that are shifting from manufacturing towards services and must adopt high productivity and high added-value work processes if they are to survive in an increasingly competitive environment, these factors are also combined with a new emphasis on the role of knowledge itself as both a driver of change and a basic prerequisite of competitive success (for example, CEC, 1994). Typically, post-Fordist types of work in a knowledge economy are expected to involve working in smaller units, with large-scale and bureaucratic enterprises falling victim to more agile competitors; and a decline in long-term commitments within the 'psychological contract' between worker and employer (Maybe et al, 1998, pp 238-42). These trends, it is said, have disrupted inherited expectations about the likely course of one's working life, making life planning a much riskier process, and challenging sources of institutional support such as pensions, insurance and training agencies (Alheit and Dausein, 2002, p 7).

What impact do these conditions have on social relationships within the workplace? On the one hand, uncertainty and insecurity may be expected to erode those relations of trust and reciprocity that require long-term commitment and sustained experience, and are bolstered by a strong sense of self-worth (Crowther, 2004, pp 126-7). These characteristics are most unlikely to thrive in a climate of insecurity and individualistic competition (Maybe et al, 1998, p 242). To this extent, then, work-based social capital might be expected to decline as a result of tendencies towards downsizing, flexibilisation and multi-skilling.

Yet, the same trends also appear to require greater interdependency between workers, and they do so in entirely new ways. The new concepts of production are associated with increased autonomy for significant groups of workers, who have increased capacity to plan and oversee the labour process, not under the direct control and command of line managers, but as a group working across traditional boundaries (Alheit, 1994, pp 84-5; Boreham, 2002, pp 9-10). These shifts may well raise the skill component of work for such workers, including of course the skills required for working in teams across different grades and disciplines. Yrjo Engeström writes of the knowledge demands arising from 'co-configuration work', which may bring together multiple producers from a variety of different organisations, including workers from supplier networks and even clients or customers, to put together and maintain an integrated package of products and services (Engeström, 2004). The role of social capital becomes more, not less, significant, with performance resting on high trust and teamwork (OECD, 1996). However, as Alheit notes, this means in turn that relationships and identities rooted in the workplace are subject to constant renegotiation and change, as people must "independently and with increasing individual risk regulate their own occupational capabilities" by taking responsibility for learning throughout their working lives (Alheit, 1994, p 85).

New technologies have been widely associated with changes in the nature of work. They are also making themselves felt more broadly in people's everyday lives, including in the home and the community. There has been considerable debate about the impact of the new technologies, and particularly of the Internet, on social capital. The Internet has proved a rich source of metaphors – networks, flows, connectivity, the web – which both express and shape people's beliefs and assumptions about the nature of mediated relationships (Edwards et al, 2004, pp 71-7). In particular, they represent cyberspace as an 'imagined community', a place where people actively construct their identities as parts of a wider set of shared relationships. For some, this is primarily an emancipatory process. According to Manuel Castells (1996), the new technologies are helping to erode the rigid identities of industrial modernism, based on class and nation, so that people in a network society are able to draw on a wide variety of contacts and values in building their sense of who they are. Others take a more negative view of the corrosive power of the Internet. Francis Fukuyama, for example, has argued that relations mediated through the digital technologies are incompatible with the creation of social capital, because they "neglect one critical factor: trust, and the shared ethical norms that underlie it" (Fukuyama, 1995, p 25). Putnam is more guarded in his judgement, not least because the Internet is still in its infancy, but he is nonetheless extremely sceptical of claims that online relationships can create reciprocity (Putnam, 2000, pp 172-7). Until recently, however, there has been more speculation on this subject than evidence. However, a whole series of studies since the late 1990s has started to suggest that, while online relationships are certainly different from face-to-face connections, they are certainly not alternatives.

On the contrary: most survey-based evidence shows that those people who are most active online tend already to have plenty of face-to-face connections, and they are complementing these by online interaction rather than replacing them (Field, 2003a, pp 102-6). Sherry Turkle's participant studies suggest that, when people go online, their public identities are more fluid and experimental than when they interact in face-to-face contexts, although the extent of this flexibility is probably overestimated by the identity-swappers themselves (Turkle, 1997, pp 177-84). So, perhaps all we can say at this stage is that the Internet appears to be associated with greater reflexivity and experimentation with the self, which can only work for actors themselves if they are engaging in relationships with others. Misztal and Urry appear to be correct in suggesting that co-presence, however intermittent, plays an important role in reducing ambiguity (and hence the scope for identity experimentation) and increasing mutual knowledge and understanding; while physical distance can help in overcoming the limitations of close ties (Misztal, 2000, pp 135-6; Urry, 2002).

Broadly, then, people's social networks do indeed appear to be changing significantly. This brief survey has provided indications of change in family relations, civic engagement, workplace connections and mediated networks. In each case, powerful elements of continuity remain. New family types turn out to resemble the old ones (not least in the persistence of patriarchy); mediated networks appear to provide social capital resources most effectively when underpinned with episodes of co-presence. Trades union membership may be falling across Europe and North America, but it is still counted in tens of millions; and, despite downsizing and multi-tasking, many people's jobs are characterised by grinding routine. Nevertheless, while avoiding the temptations of hyperbole, these four areas of analysis all provide evidence of long-term shifts in people's relationships, away from long-term commitments and towards a pattern of more conditional, reflexive and provisional arrangements.

For some writers, such as Richard Sennett, the individualisation process, combined with the informalisation of everyday life, is inherently risky because it threatens the fabric of individual character (Sennett, 1999). Yet, I have argued elsewhere that, in many respects, the more provisional and experimental nature of everyday relationships may in some respect be more favourable than inauspicious for social capital (Field, 2003a, p 113). What is clear is that these are indeed areas where our lives are undergoing a marked transformation. Just as the idea of the 'normal biography' or standard life course has been displaced by a more complex, pluralistic and variegated view of the individual biography, so it is clear that people's connections are harder to categorise simply because they are diffuse, varied, adaptable and no longer automatically bound to blood, place and job. This set of shifts in turn has marked and profound implications for people's learning; before exploring this issue, however, I return to the more general question of how people's learning is shaped by their social networks.

Changing networks and their impact on learning

Until recently, it would not have made much sense to worry about changing social networks in the context of discussions about learning. The dominant models of learning tend to be highly individualistic, and somewhat depoliticised. Even though there is increasing acknowledgement of the range of learning that people undertake, with growing attention to informal and incidental learning, attempts to develop social models of learning remain underdeveloped. Nevertheless, the development of such concepts as situated learning, activity theory and collective competence testifies to a growing interest in the ways in which learning can be viewed as the property of groups and not simply as individuals.

Probably the best known social theory of learning is associated with Lave and Wenger's concept of situated learning (Lave and Wenger, 1991). Their theory of situated cognition emphasises the way in which people acquire new skills and knowledge, and also create new frameworks of meaning, through a process of "legitimate peripheral participation" in a given "community of practice". In other words, when people join a community with a recognised, defined status as a newcomer, they learn by observing, copying and speaking with existing members of that community, some of whom may be little more advanced in their membership than the newcomers.

For Lave and Wenger, this conception helps to explain the way in which people can transmit tacit knowledge, and pass on skills that are deeply embedded in otherwise unquestioned habitual practices. Also, these features make their theory particularly attractive in the context of wider debates about the knowledge economy, where attention is paid not only to readily transmissible knowledge in its most abstract and easily codifiable forms, but to the passing on of more contextualised and fuzzy forms of 'know how'. Lave and Wenger's work may also have acquired greater significance in a context where older forms of socialisation have started to disappear; formal apprenticeship systems, for instance, have fallen victim to labour market deregulation in a number of countries, at a time when the practical challenges of inducting new workers are probably even more pressing and complex than before.

A somewhat more elaborate approach to situated cognition can be found in the work of Yrjo Engeström. Engeström's work draws heavily on Vygostky, an early Soviet social psychologist who suggested that much learning takes place in what he called the "zone of proximal development" – that is, close by and in relationship with those who have mastered a particular practice, but not necessarily under their control or even their leadership, at least in any formal sense. Engeström took this work as a point of departure for continuing to develop what Vygotsky called "activity theory", the basic principles of which are that human labour must be understood as an integrated system, incorporating activity, a set of tasks oriented towards a particular object, and which is mediated by tools that embody a particular culture. Engeström notes, among other factors, the difficulty faced by work teams in deciding what precisely the object of their activity is, and notes the importance of 'contradictions' and dialogue in reaching solutions, revising them and moving on (Engeström, 2004).

Livingstone and Sawchuk (2004, pp 55-9) note that Engeström's concept of systemic contradictions has Marxist roots, and that he sees contradictions as encouraging people to question existing accepted practice. They also note that his work emphasises the importance of alternative standpoints in providing a heterogeneity of expertise, which encourages people to consider a wider range of options than they might have done if surrounded only by like-minded others (Livingstone and Sawchuk, 2004, p 60). Yet perhaps we should not draw dramatic conclusions from Engeström's continued borrowings from Marxism. Acknowledging the benefits of variety and unexpected tensions in promoting learning is one thing;

predicting the victory of the proletariat in a future class war is quite another. And Engeström's influence has been far-reaching, not only in educational theory, but also in the field of professional business practice; to quote Livingstone and Sawchuk (2004, p 60) once more, activity theory has been at least partly "domesticated", and applied to considerable effect in exploiting the proletariat.

Nevertheless, activity does go beyond Lave and Wenger in a number of ways, not least in avoiding a tendency to oversimplification. It acknowledges conflict between members of a community as not only inevitable, at least where there are different interests at stake, but also as leading towards collective learning. Some situated cognition theorists acknowledge conflicts of interest, and acknowledge the interplay of hierarchy and knowledge involved in peripheral participation. Miriam Zukas and Janice Malcolm, for example, point out that certain communities of practice may use the peripheral status of the learner to keep newcomers on the margins, and transmit only technical and instrumental knowledge (Zukas and Malcolm, 2000). While some social cognition theorists may have been domesticated, others are not.

While they differ in several respects, though, these emerging social models of learning share a number of common features. In particular, they place an emphasis upon interdependency, communication, reciprocity and values as central prerequisites for learning. Theories of situated cognition are designed to address the ways in which people acquire and apply new information, skills and ideas by virtue of their membership of a community. This emphasis means that changes in the nature of communities are, potentially, rich with implications for learning. Furthermore, in a knowledge economy and reflexive society, learning itself becomes a constitutive ingredient of workplace performance and indeed of everyday societal life. These general reflections can be illustrated with the example of family life, which may exemplify the ways in which changes in social capital and learning are interrelated.

Family, as we have seen, plays a central role in the classical social capital literature, which has explored in detail the role of networks and values in respect of school attainment. We have also seen that family arrangements, like other intimate relationships, are becoming more fluid and open, and rely ever less on fixed structures with clear divisions between domestic and public spaces. Demographic changes such as declining numbers of children and growing numbers of older adults are also affecting family arrangements, as are the growing presence of women in post-school education and paid employment. From Coleman's perspective, these new arrangements are disastrous for social capital because they reduce stability, dissolve tie density and replace social closure by unpredictability and openness, leading ultimately to a collapse in the "social capital on which societal functioning has depended" (Coleman, 1991, p 9).

In part, these conclusions follow logically from Coleman's view of social capital as a form of social control, a hidden hand that depends on closure for its effects. As we have seen in the case of Northern Ireland, there is considerable merit in this argument in so far as it concerns the behaviour of school children. Yet Morgan, on the basis of US data, suggests that social closure among parents is only effective in fostering academic achievements among younger pupils, and is much less so – or may even have a negative influence – among high-school students. He concludes that this pattern is partly caused by the fact that communities with dense cognate ties do not invest as much in heterogeneous information as do communities with a variety of non-cognate ties, and this information is critical in providing high-school students with a horizon-expanding environment that motivates them to learn (Morgan, 2000, p 594).

Similar considerations apply to learning within the family, where changing arrangements, combined with the rapid development of new technologies and the reflexivity of daily life, introduce new forms of socialisation. Some are highly individualised, such as the learning that follows the discovery of a partner's adultery: as well as learning that 'love hurts', the loss of trust and breakdown of expectations of reciprocity can also be accompanied by distancing from friends and some kin, particularly if talk about the adultery is taboo (perhaps for fear of embarrassment, or as a result of agreed secrecy). The result is isolation, all the harder for occurring within the framework of family bonds.

Other trends are less individualised. Conventionally seen as flowing down the family tree, from adults to children, the flow of socialisation within contemporary families is increasingly multi-directional. Inverse socialisation, for example, may range from the still unusual case of children and young people serving as care-givers for dependent adults, generally an incapacitated single parent (Dearden and Becker, 1998), to the much more common and routine transmission of IT skills from children to adults (Cochinaux and de Woot, 1995). Horizontal socialisation is diversified as a result of having step-siblings, which increases the range of influences and information available to the young person.

Moreover, in a society of multiple and shifting identities, the very lack of fixed coordinates within the family may serve as a far more appropriate preparation for adulthood than did the stability and security of the 'traditional' family. However, Jamieson is probably right to ask whether fluid intimate relationships provide a sufficiently robust basis for initial identity formation among the young, and she also suggests that they may even prove damaging for adults' capacity for reciprocity and lasting cooperation (Jamieson, 1988, p 155). The aim of this discussion of family, though, is not to provide a balance sheet of the positive and negative consequences of social change, but rather to illustrate the ways in which the shifting composition of family social capital can also realign the cognitive resources that family members create and share.

Rather similar points might be made about the other three areas in which I have illustrated the overall processes of social change. In the case of civic engagement, for instance, it is clear that the main bases of social purpose adult education in Europe have gone into secular decline. The 19th-century social movements that inspired the foundation of civic adult education all entered the 20th century full of optimism and ambition; trades unions, socialist parties, temperance organisations and women's national interest groups were all critical in the promotion and support of adult education; since the creation of the welfare state, all have lost members, and their internal life is remarkably impoverished (for an example, see Seyd and Whiteley, 1992). Correspondingly, such institutional vehicles of civic adult education as the Workers' Educational Association have either gone into crisis or have found new roles (admittedly, these sometimes incorporate elements of their old identity, but this is arguably more of a legitimating device than anything else). Newer social movements, such as environmentalism, contemporary feminism or the anti-globalisation movement, appear to have very powerful capacities for self-education, and indeed find their members largely among the most highly educated; as movements, they make few if any demands on the formal educational institutions (Field, 1991).

The transformation of work, on the other hand, has multiple and direct consequences for the education and training system. This is partly because there has been growth in forms of work that deal directly with knowledge. Knowledge workers are particularly likely, it seems, to work long hours, with risks both to their health and their social capital, and they are also more likely to be engaged in teleworking which can create isolation (CEC, 2003, p 35). Yet, at the same time, knowledge-intensive work, including telework, can greatly enhance family learning, not least by providing information and ideas that come through bridging links from outside the workers' own family and neighbours (CEC, 2003, p 35). On the other hand, they often prefer to learn new skills from their fellow workers, and actively seek out positions where they are constantly presented with new problems to solve.

Knowledge workers are atypical in many respects, but we have already seen that autonomy and self-direction appear to be general features of the post-Fordist organisation of work. Of course, these features can also provide an opportunity for social capital resources to be mobilised in resistance to pressures from above, including demands that workers should learn. These developments may not always represent the sunnier side of social capital: an Australian study of attitudes towards safety among mineworkers showed that informal workplace networks generally enjoyed higher trust than did perceived outsiders (including trainers), and could often subvert messages that were seen as coming from above, resulting in serious injury to some of those involved (Somerville and Abrahamsson, 2003, p 25). This case is particularly instructive in that it underlines two facets of contemporary capitalist work. First, the fact that industrial manual work still exists on a large scale should remind us of the persistence of class inequalities. Second, though, groups such as miners are a minority of contemporary workers, and they will no longer serve as the 'archetypical proletarians' (Harrison, 1978) who occupy a symbolic space at the forefront of the organised working class. Rather, they are more and more an exception, and in some of the economically advanced countries, like Britain, they have virtually disappeared. With them has gone the stereotypical social milieu of the mining community, with the entire social life of the village centring on the pit.

German approaches to social milieu analysis

Mining and coalminers are simply one example of the steady erosion over recent decades of the connection between work, relationships, values and lifestyle. Nor is this shift confined to the old manual working class, or even to the working class: British football hooligans during the 2004 European Cup came from all social strata, and not just from an oppressed and disaffected proletariat. The tendency for socioeconomic position and values/lifestyle to be progressively uncoupled and pluralised is a general one (albeit far from ubiquitous or complete), affecting all classes, and particularly the young.

One suggestive set of studies has been undertaken in Germany (2000), which has considerable relevance to the analysis of the consequences of this change. A series of researchers (Alheit, 1994, 1996; Barz and Tippelt, 1998; Barz, 2000; Schemmann and Reinecke, 2002) has analysed participation in adult learning in the wider context of people's 'social milieus' – that is, social groupings made up of people who share to some extent a broadly similar objective position (occupation, income, housing, and so on) and agree basically on their core values and beliefs. This body of work is clearly and very explicitly influenced by Bourdieu's work on habitus, distinction and taste (Bourdieu, 1984), as well as the interests of market researchers in identifying 'niche' groups who share a common style of life, and it also draws to some extent on Max Weber's theories of social class.

The social milieu approach was first used to investigate adult learning in a study commissioned by the Friedrich-Ebert-Stiftung, an educational foundation closely allied to the Social Democratic Party, in an attempt to discover how it might halt the long-term decline in demand for political education (Barz and Tippelt, 1998, p 528). Using a model that distinguished nine broad sociocultural milieus, the researchers showed clear differences in terms of demand for particular leisure activities, cultural experiences and learning opportunities, including strong variations in preferences for the content, location and timing of learning activities. Subsequently, this broad model has been adopted in a number of studies of participation in adult learning. Although it differs from the approach adopted in this volume, there are strong parallels between social capital analysis and social milieu analysis. A brief summary of the German studies may therefore be helpful.

The underlying questions for the German studies were concerned with how the habitus was changing for different groups of people, and whether these changes were connected with changes in occupational and economic structures. Preliminary qualitative studies of habitus types were then supplemented by a factor analysis of responses to a set of some 44 indicators in order to establish the main habitus groupings to which people belong (Vester et al, 2001; Vester, 2005). Typical habitus types – or social milieus – included the following (Barz, 2000):

1. 'Upper Conservative Milieu' (some 8% of the population, and static), characterised by high incomes and a higher than average formal education; the main aspirations were material success and social recognition, and the lifestyle centred on family, traditionalism, quality, authenticity and good taste.
2. 'Petit-Bourgeois Milieu' (21%, and falling), mostly with medium or smaller incomes and usually a solid secondary education followed by vocational training; this group aspired to independence, and its lifestyle was typically conventional, conservative and restrained.
3. 'Traditional Blue Collar Milieu' (5%, and falling), including a high proportion of older workers and pensioners, usually completing vocational training after school, aiming at material security and recognition in the immediate social circle, with a preference for solid and lasting products.
4. 'Uprooted Blue Collar Milieu' (12%, and growing), often experiencing periods of unemployment and possessing few or no formal qualifications, wishing to keep up with the middle class, and mostly living in the present.

5. 'Progressive No Collar Workers Milieu' (6%, and growing), relatively youthful and often in skilled work or public service employment, tolerant of different life styles, open to new experiences, prepared for change, and focused on leisure time.
6. 'Social Climbers Milieu' (25%, and growing), usually qualified at secondary educational level, and often skilled workers or self-employed/freelance, with medium to high incomes, aiming at advancement and recognition, and desiring prestigious high status goods.
7. 'Technocratic Liberal Milieu' (9%, and static), well educated, including many established civil servants and prosperous self-employed/freelance, affluent, and aiming at success and a high living standard; lifestyle linked to desire for self-expression, open to new trends, life not to be taken too seriously.
8. 'Hedonistic Milieu' (12%, and growing) usually with little formal education, aged mainly 15-30, small to medium incomes, aiming to live intensively for the here and now and escape from the banal demands of everyday life, fascination with luxury and consumption, impulse shopping.
9. 'Alternative Milieu' (2%, and decreasing), highly educated, many students, public service professionals, freelancers, and wide range of incomes; aiming at self-realisation, rejecting materialism, environmentally conscious, and deliberately alternative.

Although this schema has undergone change in recent years, partly in response to German unification and partly in response to further evidence of cultural change (with the 'alternatives' disappearing, and the identification of a distinctively 'postmodern milieu', for instance), this brief sketch provides a reasonable basis for judging the value of the model.

In a recent attempt to apply this model to adult learning, Heiner Barz and Rudolf Tippelt made a small number of adjustments designed to tease out the influence of factors such as life stage and experiences of schooling (Barz and Tippelt, 1998; Barz, 2000). In terms of method, they opted to use 120 in-depth interviews rather than surveying larger numbers with a standardised questionnaire. Confining their initial study of the Freiburg region to women, and to learning in the context of *Volkshochschulen* (local adult education centres), Barz and Tippelt nevertheless found that the different social milieus displayed markedly varying attitudes towards adult learning. Interest in the *Volkshochschulen* was particularly high among the 'social climbers' (who were looking for qualifications, health/fitness and creativity classes), the 'progressive no collar workers' (who were broadly enthusiastic about lifelong learning in general, and looked to the *Volkshochschulen* for vocational courses), the 'petit-bourgeois' group (who understood education as a widening of one's own cultural horizons), and the 'technocratic liberal' group (who had a broad range of interests). Outright hostility was expressed only by the 'hedonistic' group, who found it boring, and thought of the *Volkshochschulen* as a social activity or cultural activity for the young. The 'upper conservative' milieu felt that adult education was a good thing, but for other people (though many older people from this group already attend classes), as did the 'uprooted blue collar workers'.

Clearly, the social milieu model differs from the approach taken in this book. Compared with the concept of social capital, the notion of social milieu is both broader and narrower. In its scope, the concept of 'social milieu' is a much wider one than social capital, since it embraces both people's objective socioeconomic position and the core values and beliefs that they hold. At the same time, the idea of social milieu is largely a descriptive one, rather than claiming the kind of theoretical status that is held for the concept of social capital. The idea of social milieu as developed by Barz and others is used largely to provide a schematic basis for categorising different groups' sociocultural attitudes in relation to their socioeconomic class situation. This has important implications for the way that this idea is then used to study attitudes towards learning. Since attitudes towards learning can be seen as subsets of wider beliefs and values, the analysis is somewhat circular: if one distinguishing feature of a group is the set of norms that shape its style of life, then little wonder if these norms are also reflected in respect of attitudes towards learning. Theories of social capital, by contrast, imply that the existence of a specific range of social connections, and the quality of these connections, serve as a set of resources that will affect – and therefore help to explain – access to information, skills and other knowledge assets.

So far, social milieu approaches have not received the attention they deserve in the English-speaking world. Partly this is because little has been available in English until recently (but see Barz and Tippelt, 1998; Vester, 2005). However, an intriguing Australian study of market segmentation in demand for and attitudes to training and lifelong learning has adopted methods that are partly comparable to those of the German social milieu researchers (Research Forum, 2000). This study, commissioned for the Australian National Training Authority (ANTA), similarly used factor analysis and cluster analysis to examine people's attitudes towards learning and their plans for future learning. Having established the existence of eight broad clusters based on different combinations of key indicators of attitudes and behavioural intentions, the researchers then examined the socioeconomic position of the individuals that fell within each cluster. However, the typology rested more on headline images than a serious attempt to locate people within a specific milieu. Thus it included 'Passionate learners' (21%) who value learning and are highly likely themselves to learn in the future. This group enjoyed middle incomes, were disproportionately female and under-45, metropolitan, professional/ managerial and well educated already. Its learning preferences included IT, culture, health care and management. Other groups identified included 'Almost There', 'Learn to Earn' and 'Forget it' (8%), a group of people who are simply uninterested in learning, feel it has been of little benefit in the past, and are generally happy with their lot. This last segment is disproportionately male and in the age groups between 25 and 64, non-metropolitan, without a university degree, and in manual work. Its members show some interest in gaining and building IT skills (Research Forum, 2000, pp 12-28).

The ANTA study shares some of the flaws of the work inspired by Vester, and adds some that are all its own. It is considerably more descriptive, as the various categories used – which are obviously those of market research – make no pretence at explaining the patterns that they report. Yet, like the German milieu studies, the ANTA findings clearly demonstrate that attitudes do fall into broad patterns (or clusters), and these are broadly related to people's socioeconomic positions. The ANTA study lacks the theoretical sophistication of the German work, it steers clear from the wider socioeconomic context, and it is also missing the sense of change over time that Vester and his collaborators have shown. It might be best to see the German studies as offering the most promising approach, particularly where we are seeking to explore the relationship between people's connections and values on the one hand, and their engagement with learning on the other.

Despite the qualifications sketched above, I believe that there is considerable merit in this approach. It accepts (and shows) that class distinctions persist, but the different classes are increasingly subdivided by life style, as well as by the extent to which they see themselves as the winners or the losers of modernisation, and some lifestyle patterns tend to cross class boundaries. Thus, established class cultures may remain stable, not least because they remain effective at enabling their members to cope with the everyday impact of social and economic change – up to a point. However, their appeal is diminishing, and Vester's team (Vester et al, 2001) also believes it likely that the effectiveness of class-based cultures – whether elite or subordinate – may also be declining. While the result at the top is the stranding of once-privileged subgroups who can no longer rely on exclusive club memberships to maintain their standing, for instance, lower down the social scale the consequences are intensified exclusion and isolation for those who rely on union and neighbourly solidarity to see them through. Vester and his colleagues have also shown that class-based cultures have lost much of their meaning for key parts of the population, including many young people.

Despite the remarkable persistence of social inequalities, then, the ties of class-based social milieus and classical fixed mentalities have loosened. The resulting pluralisation of social networks has in turn increased the already rapid rate of growth in the array of information and ideas that people can access, leading to further increases in the range of choices and options that are not only available but actually required. The outcomes of these decisions then produce further realignments in the social contexts in which learning takes place. The result is, inevitably, considerable complexity in the ways in which social learning occurs.

Complexity and social change

In developing his concept of collective competence, Boreham has rightly stressed the role of discourse within activity systems (Boreham, 2004, p 10). We could go further: in order to constitute oneself and others as an imagined community, which thus embraces those who are not known directly or encountered routinely, people use talk. Among Australian miners, for instance, storytelling is used to support a culture of "unsafe behaviour by normalising it through joking"; the use of protective gear incurred sanctions, with the wearer being taunted as a 'tart' (Somerville and Abrahamsson, 2003, pp 25-6). This occurred in a dangerous job where people knew that they might depend on one another's collective competence for survival. The miners sought to downplay stress and fear through a mixture of humour, masculinity and the exercise of control, all of which evoked and were embedded in talk.

Stephen Ball has similarly emphasised the role of talk in the case of middle-class parents seeking to promote the positional advantages of their children (Ball, 2003). When identifying and pursuing a school place that will endow one's child with significant positional advantages, middle-class parents pursue individualist goals by accessing communal information, particularly through 'grapevine information', which is communicated informally:

> The middle class, the chattering classes, are adept at these forms of talk. They use talk in a variety of domestic and social contexts, to get things done and to establish and maintain collective identity. This kind of talk, the skills of questioning in particular, and other social competencies, are part of their cultural capital.

> They are used to presenting themselves and evaluating others through talk. (Ball, 2003, p 64)

It is through their networks that middle-class people access and judge 'hot knowledge' about the reputation, routines and achievements of local schools, which then allows them to place into perspective the 'cold knowledge' that appears in more formal arenas, such as the school or college prospectus (Ball, 2003, p 100).

The middle-class parents are deploying a highly individualised form of collective competence (Boreham, 2004). Yet the collective competences of the miners also arise from the interplay of mutual dependency and shared values that are developed through collective problem solving, and articulated through a shared language. What is also interesting about both cases is the way in which class identities clearly persist, and are constantly worked on and developed through discourse.

The interplay between networks and learning is not simply part of a process by which skills and techniques are shared, and information is passed around. It is also an active part of the process of making sense of the world, by talking about feelings in complex and apparently contradictory ways. The work of Somerville and Abrahamsson (2003) and Ball (2003) suggests that discourse is a key material practice in enabling people to exchange and create knowledge through network interactions. Yet talk matters most where the relationships in which it occurs are valued ones, underpinned by shared values and bolstered in the longer term by broad expectations of reciprocity. These features can be found in the stereotypically traditional proletarian setting of coalmining, as well as among the epitome of the mobile new middle classes, Ball's suburban middle-class mothers.

These examples are used for illustrative purposes, to show that the new and changing features of our social arrangements are continuing to serve as collective resources, but in ways that are themselves subject to and part of the wider processes of change. They turn out to be extremely complex, but it is hardly surprising if the broad thrust of change is to create types of social capital that are looser and more open than the closed loops of bonding social capital analysed by Coleman. Moreover, while Putnam's model of social capital is certainly looser than Coleman's, it remains somewhat ahistorical, and even shows a distinct tinge of nostalgia for the lost world of the 1950s and early 1960s.

We should remember that Americans do not really 'bowl alone'. People may have stopped joining clubs, and bowling in organised teams on a regular basis as part of a local league. But, instead of booking a lane for themselves to play in isolation, they behave like the characters of the

Coen brothers' wonderful film, *The Big Lebowski*, arranging to meet a bunch of friends, and making an evening of it which involves bowling, wine or beer and pizza. What is gained, apart from anything else, is playing with people whom you like and whose company you enjoy – a reminder that Putnam generally ignores the importance of affect, that obvious and simple ingredient in contemporary relationships. This has much larger consequences for our understanding of the role of social ties in enabling cooperation in a knowledge economy and reflexive society.

Social capital in reflexive modernity is itself a powerful form of learning, which occurs in a range of settings that are inherently characterised by complexity. This raises serious questions about how we find our way around the new social maze, constantly changing as it is around us as a consequence of our own decisions and the decisions of countless others. Barbara Misztal, for example, has pointed out that the loosening up of habitual deference, along with an increasing willingness to challenge hierarchical forms of social organisation, by increasing the scope of choice and decision making by individuals and organisations, has also enhanced "the practical importance of various non-hierarchical, voluntary negotiated forms of self-co-ordination" (Misztal, 2000, p 124). Moreover, in a complex and interdependent society, the costs of opportunism and a generalised caution (or 'pre-caution') are so great as to place a premium on access to such resources as commitment and trust, which she believes to be situated in "network-like relationships" that emerge within and across the boundaries of organisations and hierarchies (Misztal, 2000, pp 125-6).

In contemporary societies, people do not belong to a fixed circle of kin, neighbours, workmates and friends. In her longitudinal analysis of adults in the Portland region of Oregon, Clare Strawn notes that: "People are usually part of multiple social networks and discourse communities", and different groups will also adopt different strategies for engaging with their own specific situation (Strawn, 2002). This inevitably leads to complex outcomes for those involved. Strawn sought to resolve the conceptual challenge posed by this complexity by adopting a form of discourse analysis, dividing specific groups into those who belong to 'the dominant discourse community' and those who are part of the 'subordinate discourse community'. From this, she deduces that marginalised communities might deploy their social capital to tackle barriers by sharing affective and instrumental resources like information. Yet social networks might also pose new barriers, such as conformity to the demands of family, neighbourhood and workplace, abusive relationships that limit autonomy, and 'negative valuation of endeavors' (Strawn, 2002). Such complex patterns mean that social networks can both promote learning and try to control and limit learning and its consequences. As Portes puts it, social capital in the form of social control may clash with social capital in the form of "network-mediated benefits", since the latter may consist precisely of "the ability to bypass existing norms" (Portes, 1998, p 13).

Scholarly debates over lifelong learning and social capital are producing new questions at least as quickly as others are being answered. It seems reasonably certain that social capital and lifelong learning are intertwined with one another, but the precise nature of the connections clearly depends upon a large number of different factors. In particular, we need to recognise that we live in a fast-moving, reflexive and highly dynamic world, with complex interplays of continuity and change in different elements at different times. Researchers also need to remember the deep continuities of the '*longue durée*'.

Socioeconomic inequality along social class lines is one element of the *longue durée*. Capitalism has not gone away, and neither have the deep inequalities of power and well-being that fall along the familiar lines of social class. I follow Stephen Ball in seeing class in Weberian rather than Marxist terms, with issues of distribution and exchange playing their part alongside production and the exploitation of labour (Ball, 1993). Within this active process of construction of class and other inequalities, social capital and lifelong learning can be either cause, effect or process. At one extreme, moreover, they may well reinforce each other: those with the least valued forms of social capital may have little reliable information about new skills and knowledge, and may receive active misinformation about the nature and relevance of new learning opportunities. This in turn reinforces a pattern of low expectations, so that learning and connections are both forced into a coping strategy that aims to deal with 'what is', rather than an active strategy aiming to move towards 'what might be'. But this is to take a simple and clear model of the connections, which are far more commonly characterised by unevenness and complexity.

Dynamism and innovation are also key parts of capitalism's *longue durée*. Talk of the knowledge economy since the 1980s (as of the technological society in the 1960s) tends to forget or ignore the fact that capitalism is an inherently dynamic economic system. From the earliest stages of the industrial revolution, ideas and skills were spread by personal contact as well as through the new mass media of cheap newsprint and affordable, portable illustrated textbooks, manuals, dictionaries and encyclopedias. Direct contact was made possible partly by the existence of modernised transport systems, but also and more routinely by what today might be called clustering. But it was a clustering where production (including discovery and invention of new processes and techniques) took place within a walk or a ride of the home. People who lived in the same town or city could take time to visit their competitors, drink with the rest of the supply chain and dine with their customers. Jenny Uglow has vividly described the world of Birmingham's Lunar Society, an 18th-century group of scientists, industrialists, engineers and designers who met monthly on the night of the full moon, the better to find their way home (Uglow, 2003). But this was only one example, if a somewhat remarkable one, of a much more common tendency (Szreter, 2000). By the late 19th century, such intimacy was becoming less straightforward. As commuting, specialisation and the separation of ownership from economic administration started to erode the conditions that had made the Lunar Society possible, so routine interpersonal connection served less and less as the basis for sharing ideas, skills and information.

In short, it may well be that current social change is producing precisely those types of social capital that are most directly associated with dynamic, heterodox learning. Philip Cooke has argued that the high economic growth rate shown by the Republic of Ireland since the 1970s may well have been promoted by skills creation and innovation processes, but these owed little to bonding social capital in a Catholic country with relatively low levels of trust, high levels of individualism, and an associational life dominated until recently by the church. Cooke also discounts the effect of government policies designed to promote clustering and social partnership, since in a small country with a limited home market there are not enough scale effects to trigger high levels of business networking. Rather, Cooke suggests, the Irish Republic's skills and innovation systems are the product of foreign direct investment and other external influences such as the European Union (Cooke, 2002, pp 89-91). Perhaps this goes too far, for the Irish Republic remains a small country with a high level of interpersonal connections; like many small countries and island states, people in the Irish Republic often know and deal with one another in multiple capacities; a country that was a colony less than a century ago is also unlikely to show high levels of trust in institutions that, historically, were thought of as the preserve of the invader. And – a point that Cooke neglects – it has by European standards a young population, with a ready supply of fresh labour and a willingness to accept new ideas. Rather than discounting the Irish Republic's social capital, then, we might consider the possibility that it possesses precisely the type of networks that promote innovation and rapid learning (and unlearning).

If it is true that the rules of social engagement have changed, and are increasingly flexible and tolerant or even promoting of informality, then formal guides to etiquette – of the kind that became increasingly popular as the rigidities of feudalism were replaced by the fluidities of industrial capitalism – start to lose their value. Also, in so far as people are tied ever more loosely to wider social milieus and mentalities associated with particular socioeconomic classes (Alheit, 1994; Barz, 2000), it is no longer enough to rely on the classical 'cultural capital' that, according to Bourdieu, determines the persistence of existing social structures (Bourdieu, 1986). As Barbara Misztal notes, people need to be more reflexive and active in acquiring the skills and knowledge needed in order to 'read' a more fluid and open social order: "To ensure safe passage and to prove one's knowledge of the rules, one needs to develop increasingly sophisticated skills of reading and interpreting symbols and signs that others exhibit in everyday life" (Misztal, 1996, p 116).

The nature and requirements of such a 'social literacy' are among a number of issues discussed in the next chapter, which considers the practical implications of some of the broad patterns and trends discussed so far.

FIVE

What next?

Writing in a forum closely associated with New Labour, Simon Szreter proposed that social capital could "offer critical assistance to the putative Third Way by providing it with its own distinctive political economy" (Szreter, 1999, p 30). Szreter acknowledged that social capital was a "double-edged sword", with networks capable of excluding and dominating as well as including and emancipating. Nevertheless, the thrust of his article argued that the benefits of multiple ties – particularly weak ties – were accentuated in a modern competitive world market. The task for government was therefore to invest in measures that would produce more social capital and civic participation, as a means of avoiding the twin extremes of the free market and a strong state (Szreter, 1999). A rather more inflated assertion appeared on the front cover of the magazine in which Szreter's paper appeared: "Social capital could come to be seen as important as the Keynesian revolution, in providing an alternative theoretical and practical guide to the economy".

Szreter's are strong claims indeed, and they are treated in this chapter with a mixture of scepticism and sympathy. In my own brief experience as a policy adviser to New Labour[1], I found that it is much easier to knock down other people's policy prescriptions than develop your own. If I adopt a more cautious approach than Simon Szreter, this is not because I believe government should do nothing about social capital, or lifelong learning. On the contrary. Doing nothing is all too plainly a prescription for doing something, but on the basis of neglect rather than design. This book has shown repeatedly that social capital has consequences for learning, and that learning has consequences for social capital. Those consequences are not always clear cut, nor are they perhaps generally as powerful as other factors such as socioeconomic position. Nevertheless, people's networks affect their ability to exchange ideas and information, and provide a bedding that nurtures their affective capabilities (see also Heenan, 2002; Cloonan, 2004). Conversely, loneliness and ignorance also affect the lives of those who lack social support mechanisms, who are given fewer and less reliable opportunities to acquire and build new knowledge and skills. These things matter, and policy makes a difference – as do the professional practices of people who deliver services (including education) and allocate resources. At the very least, the research summarised and discussed in this book should give us some notion of what not to do!

Yet both social capital and lifelong learning are difficult customers. They present policy makers with tightly interwoven bundles of fuzzy, complex and multidimensional issues. It is highly likely that some interventions – however well intentioned – will have unintended consequences. Moreover, although social capital appears to have an influence on learning, it seems to be no more significant – and possibly less so – than social class or direct educational investment, and we should not overplay our hand by exaggerating its impact. So, accepting the need for caution and care, how should we proceed? What, it might be asked, is to be done? And, in particular, are any clear policy lessons to be found in the complex and heavily nuanced findings of the Northern Ireland research reported in the early chapters of this volume? Before answering these questions, though, I will take some space to present the reasons for my scepticism.

Faltering first steps?

Policies for lifelong learning and social capital are not as new as the language might suggest. The discourse itself may be relatively new, as we have seen, with both terms surging to the forefront of policy attention in the 1990s. The language of social capital attracted wider attention in the mid-1990s, after Putnam published a paper with the title 'Bowling Alone' (Putnam, 1995); the language of lifelong learning also first became widespread in the 1990s, particularly with the proposal to declare a European Year of Lifelong Learning (CEC, 1994). If the language is new, though, many existing practices and policies are clearly relevant to the discussion. Inevitably, this must raise the question of whether the new concepts will prove as revolutionary in terms of policy and practice as their enthusiasts claim.

At this stage, of course, it is too early to say what impact the new concepts are likely to make. Lifelong learning became a leitmotif of education policy debate in the mid-1990s, and remains a key goal of educational modernisers in intergovernmental bodies such as the OECD or the European Commission, as well as influencing policy in a number of the advanced capitalist nations. In most of its guises, lifelong learning policy has centrally addressed the goals of economic competitiveness and social cohesion, both of which are also core policy concerns of the social capital debate.

Social capital's advance has been more modest. While numerous Green Papers and similar policy documents have been published under the heading of lifelong learning, social capital has so far belonged more to the less public worlds of the seminar or briefing paper. Nonetheless, the concept has been widely discussed in some policy circles, including the mainstream of New Labour in Britain. Putnam himself has held intensive discussions with both the Bush administration and its predecessor; while the European Commission has so far been relatively slow to explore policies on social capital, Putnam has also run seminars for a number of European governments, including Bertie Aherne's Fianna Fail administration in Ireland (Field, 2003a, pp 116-17).

The debate has been at its sharpest in some of the intergovernmental organisations. The OECD in particular has actively promoted both ideas, and has also encouraged member governments to consider the links between them, particularly in an influential report on human and social capital, authored largely by a civil servant on secondment from the Irish Department of Education and Science (OECD, 2001a). An expert report published by the European Commission argued that:

> ... social and human capital are *mutually reinforcing* and produce beneficial effects not only in *economic terms* (at aggregate, company and individual level) but also *socially*, in areas such as social inclusion, health and governance. Building social and human capital *is a key element on the road to the Lisbon targets* [ie, sustainable economic growth, more and better jobs and greater social cohesion]. (CEC, 2003, p 50; emphasis in original)

There has also been interest in the World Bank, where Michael Woolcock among others has sought to argue for a socially embedded approach to economic development in the Third World; this has particular importance because of the Bank's direct influence over aid recipients (Dasgupta, 2000). A number of Third World governments and charities, however, have contested the Bank's conception of social capital, arguing for a more 'bottom-up' approach to capacity building by supporting existing poor people's institutions rather than imposing new ones (Fox, 1997).

So, policy debate has developed in both fields, although so far the OECD and World Bank are unusual in acknowledging the implications of social capital and lifelong learning for each other. Elsewhere, discussions appear to have proceeded in parallel, like trains on separate tracks. The example of policy development within the European Commission provides an instructive example. For at least two decades, the wider policy agenda in the European Union has sought to balance the demands of competitiveness with the maintenance of social cohesion; as President of the Commission, Delors added to this an interest in promoting European citizenship, and this has been pursued (if intermittently) by his successors. It is not surprising, then, that the European Union policy debate has at least touched on the related issues of active citizenship, social inclusion and lifelong learning.

However, these developments have mostly taken place in different departments, and have only rarely come together in a coherent way. Thus the department responsible for education and training suggested in 2000 that: "*Lifelong learning* is no longer just one aspect of education and training; it *must become the guiding principle* for provision and participation across the full continuum of learning contexts" (CEC, 2000, p 3; emphasis in original).

The department went on to argue that the "full continuum of learning contexts" included many areas of life that had previously had no connection with education and training, but nevertheless provided opportunities for people to gain new skills and knowledge, such as civic engagement. Subsequently, as part of the work programme on education and training requested by the Council of Ministers in March 2001, the Commission created a working group to make recommendations on "the open learning environment, active citizenship, equal opportunities and social cohesion" (European Council of Ministers, 2002).

Quite separately, the Commission's directorate general for social affairs has also promoted active citizenship and engaged in dialogue with non-governmental and voluntary organisations. Indeed, the concept of social capital itself has also been adopted to examine the factors underlying economic competitiveness across the European Union, this time in the directorate general responsible for regional affairs (Mouqué, 1999, pp 63-72). Another part of the European Commission, responsible for research and technology development, has provided finance for research teams to address territorial and organisational configurations affecting the potential for innovation and economic development, including systems and networks of innovation, institutions, sectoral and regional agencies, small and large firms, and human and social capital (European Commission Directorate-General for Research, 2002, p 5).

The European Commission has, then, adopted broad policies for both lifelong learning and social capital that span different ministerial departments and seek to promote the Commission's core goals of competitiveness and cohesion.

At first sight, then, both lifelong learning and social capital are in a rather promising position. Policy makers have shown considerable interest in promoting lifelong learning, and are starting to take a similar interest in building social capital. In each case, these concepts are being adopted because policy makers – reasonably enough, it might be thought – see them as closely connected with more fundamental goals, such as social inclusion and economic growth. But, of course, it is one thing for a government to adopt an overarching policy goal and quite another to pursue it effectively.

This is partly because the process of governance is itself in flux. With nation states coming under challenge from powerful external forces (often conventionally but misleadingly described as 'globalisation') as well as internally from electorates that have turned away from the welfarist settlement of the post-1945 period, the broad thrust of governance is being turned away from direct control and delivery towards a more complex set of strategies for public management. Moreover, both social capital and lifelong learning are undertaken by and belong to citizens and other non-governmental actors (including, of course, people who work for the government) rather than government. One British scholar uses the metaphor of a boat, describing the new public management as less concerned with 'rowing' than 'steering' (Rhodes, 1996). Key features include contractual relationships for the delivery of public services, delegation of routine management within the public services, the use of indicators, benchmarking and targets, and the creation of partnerships and dialogue with key actors. Precisely the same processes that have focused attention on social capital and capabilities for learning lie at the heart of the new complexities of governance in late modern societies.

Nor is it always easy for governments to promote policies that tackle complex and interdependent issues. The very nature of social capital and lifelong learning is that they cut across the responsibilities of different government departments. As the Director of the National Institute for Adult Continuing Education pointed out, "Adults' learning opportunities regularly lie at the cusp of overlapping policy responsibilities – as family learning, learning and health and prison education testify" (Tuckett, 2001, p 10).

Yet the capacity of governmental departments for coordination is extremely limited, even in a comparatively small and new civil service such as that of the European Commission. Inter-ministerial coordination, then, is another factor that has clearly inhibited development of policy goals that span different departmental and ministerial territories.

Furthermore, measuring social capital and lifelong learning present considerable challenges to policy makers. This is particularly clear in the case of lifelong learning, which encompasses the informal exchange of tacit knowledge and embedded skills that were demonstrated in Chapter Two. Much the same might be said of social capital, which depends heavily on relations of affect (or whether people like and trust one another) and norms of reciprocity, while simultaneously nurturing people's affective capacities and shaping their individual and collective efficacy. The voices presented in Chapter Two belonged to people whose networks had developed organically, over time, and in complex ways. The knowledge assets that they accessed through their networks were bundled together in ways that were unique to them and their communities.

Sanjaya Lall has noted that conventional neoclassical economy theory, based on the paradigm of perfect competition, "shies away from dealing with widespread and diffuse externalities and fuzzy learning phenomena" (Lall, 2000, p 14). Lall was writing about social capital, but his comments might apply equally to lifelong learning. It is significant that much policy debate in respect of both concepts has accordingly concentrated on such questions as measurement and the management of partnerships (OECD, 2001a, 2001b; PIU, 2002). Yet these very emphases may incur negative unintended consequences.

Steering by performance targets and partnership management means that frontline service workers experience a combination of high risk environments and systems of performance monitoring and accountability, that reflect and embody limited trust in public service professionals. In turn, this appears to erode still further the levels of trust within the public sector workforce (Avis, 2004), as well as placing unrealistic and unresourced demands on "street-level bureaucrats" to work in new ways (Wright, 2001). This in turn creates mutual suspicion between street-level bureaucrats and the people who work with them in managed partnerships (Nixon et al, 2001, p 340).

Measurement therefore poses a considerable challenge for policy makers, who have responded with some ingenuity (see OECD, 2001a). One oft-canvassed solution is the adoption of 'soft indicators' that acknowledge the complexities of fuzzy policy concepts; but the truth is that once policy makers have defined soft indicators, they quickly become hard indicators. Another alternative is the creation of multidimensional indicators, but the use of large batteries of targets poses almost insuperable problems for those charged with monitoring and improving performance. Because they involve governments in 'steering' behaviour and influencing beliefs, in a context defined by a multiplicity of widely distributed actors and intermediaries, management by performance targets means that the risks of unintended consequences, goal distortion and even fraud are very high (Field, 2000, pp 24-30).

Furthermore, much government activity may be dressed in the language of lifelong learning or social capital, but in practice it seems that policy makers and service providers are sometimes simply re-branding existing activities. This has been obvious in the field of adult education, where many providing organisations have simply repackaged their courses under the label of lifelong learning; the courses themselves are unchanged. Similarly, governments have adopted the language of lifelong learning to describe what is actually a shift of attention away from general adult education and towards vocational training and upskilling (Rubenson, 2001). Inevitably, this provokes cynicism among fieldworkers, whose response is that they can see through the fancy new language; underneath the emperor's new clothes is, invariably, 'nothing new'. Many community development workers in Britain and Ireland have been at best wary of the language of social capital, at worst downright hostile (Morrissey and McGinn, 2001, p 17; Salmon, 2002, p 49). Social capital and lifelong learning are often both mired between the repackaging activities of the state and service providers, and the (oft well-founded) suspicions of the street-level bureaucrats.

Finally, some people believe that we should avoid such terms as social capital or lifelong learning altogether. For neo-liberals and conservatives, these phrases are simply ways of disguising plans for the state to intervene in ordinary people's private affairs. While they accept that family and community may be desirable, and that socioeconomic change demands continuous learning, they believe that the best route is for individual decisions to take their course through a free market. More radical critics believe that the terminology of social capital and lifelong learning is hopelessly contaminated by association with capitalism and/or the state (Blaxter and Hughes, 2001). Those who do use such concepts are distracting attention from the underlying material and structural causes of inequality and exclusion (McClenaghan, 2000). While neither of these groups is particularly influential in policy circles, they may have influenced some professional groups, particularly in the context of overload and scepticism described earlier.

To date, then, there has been much interest but little concrete progress in either field. As the European Commission put it in a staff memorandum on lifelong learning, "The [European] Union's member states have clearly found a large measure of consensus on their shared interest in lifelong learning, but this has not yet been translated into effective action" (CEC, 2000, p 7).

And this despite the fact that lifelong learning has received considerably more policy attention since the mid-1990s than social capital. In the light of the lack of concrete progress to date in either of the two key areas of lifelong learning and social capital, the prospects of longer-term development of policy and practice in both areas together might reasonably be judged as slim. Yet, as I have already stressed, doing nothing is itself a decision that has consequences for people's networks and how they learn. And policies that seem to have nothing to do with social capital or learning can inadvertently have massive negative effects on both, as is shown by the massive information and communication deficits that sometimes afflict those organisations whose managers embark on large-scale restructuring exercises (CIPD, 2003, pp 11-13). Given what we know about the benefits of connectedness and learning, including their benefits for one another, doing nothing is likely on balance to prove harmful.

Implications for policy and practice

After spending so much space rehearsing the reasons why policy and practice are difficult, the very idea of rebuilding community may seem laughable and, when combined with the notion of lifelong learning, even hopeless. The research findings summarised in Chapters Two and Three do not lend themselves to easy practical conclusions: the fact that gardening is associated with low participation in learning, while adultery is associated with high participation, provides at first sight a rather improbable guide to action. Even on a closer examination, I would suggest that the research evidence offers a rather difficult set of messages for policy makers and practitioners, mainly because the findings summarised here are complex ones.

Essentially, this book has suggested that social capital is an independent variable that explains some variations in learning. In summary, people's networks are learning resources, which can give them greater access to, and enhanced capabilities of using, information and skills, whether acquired through formal mechanisms such as schools or informal means such as gossip and observation. People whose social capital consists mainly of close ties, and where their bonding connections are with others who have low levels of human capital, are very likely to enjoy very limited access to ways of acquiring and generating new skills and knowledge; their network resources are usually good only at providing them with coping skills. However, social capital can in these circumstances provide a positive influence on young people, provided that people's bonding ties are integrated into wider social networks; in the case of Northern Ireland, this 'bridging by proxy' is often provided by the churches. Access to a variety of heterogeneous ties, by contrast, offers a highly effective way of accessing and generating a broad range of new knowledge and skills. Yet at the same time, heterogeneous networks may well promote types of learning that are challenging and even disruptive of existing social arrangements; precisely because they provoke innovative and creative responses, variety in networks can also cause people to ask why they maintain their involvement in particular relationships, and encourage them to explore alternatives. Finally, all these different interrelations between networks and learning are shaped and in turn shape other social forces, including socioeconomic situation and cultural norms.

So, all in all, the impact of social capital on learning is complex, and is always bound up with other factors. What looks initially like an appealingly simple slogan – 'Invest in social capital' – turns out to be a rather more difficult set of judgements and choices. What types of learning do we wish to encourage, and what type of networks should we build? What types of social capital encourage the forms of learning that are desirable, and what types hinder it? Will deliberate intervention do more good than harm, or will it inadvertently undermine the conditions under which either social capital or learning take place? And, if the research findings were not complicated enough already, few of these questions can be answered in general terms, since the specific contexts in which learning and networks interact will vary from one set of circumstances to another. But at least the focus on learning and social capital offers a way of posing the questions, and of making sure that some of the underlying concerns are addressed.

Such concerns are familiar ones to anybody involved in community development – or 'neighbourhood renewal', in the language of New Labour. Since the 1980s, community development and economic regeneration strategies have increasingly rested on a broad concept of partnership. In Scotland, for example, the devolved administration has placed considerable emphasis on the process of community planning, undertaken through Community Planning Partnerships that bring local councils and other statutory agencies together with representatives of the voluntary sector and the business community, working in consultation with local communities themselves to draft detailed definitions of public service and quality of life outcomes for their local area. In the Scottish context, as in many others, there is at least a formal recognition of the role of community learning and community development in this process:

> We see community learning and development as an effective way of working with people, through building their knowledge, skills and confidence, in order to:
>
> - tackle power and equalities issues;
> - develop community activity and organisation; and
> - exercise influence over the decisions of public organisations and others. (Scottish Executive, 2003, p 11)

Broadly similar approaches lie at the heart of the notion of learning cities and learning communities developed, among others, by the OECD and a number of regional and local government bodies in western Europe and Australasia (Faris, 2004).

However, a social capital approach to this issue provides grounds for at least questioning and possibly challenging some existing practices. In particular, the differentiated approach to social capital that I have pursued throughout this book calls into question those strategies that are designed primarily to build connections among members of a particular disadvantaged community. Here the distinction between bonding, bridging and linking forms of social capital is likely to be helpful. Traditional community development strategies tended to focus on consolidating and strengthening the network resources found within disadvantaged communities. This approach may be quite an effective way of building bonding social capital within the community, and thereby helping people to develop coping strategies. In its more radical variant, it may also provide bridging linkages to similar communities elsewhere, enabling them to organise together to advance their collective interests (Lovett, 1975). Yet it is bad at building networks that provide access to important resources that are invariably located outside such communities; such community development strategies fall short on what Woolcock calls linking ties (Woolcock, 1998). As a recent Irish policy paper concluded, this perspective also has implications for the methods used to build community capacity: "An excessive reliance on self-help and own capacity-building could mean that neighbourhoods and communities that lack the critical knowledge, social contact and internal cohesion miss out" (NESF, 2003, p 70).

Openness to external interventions and partnerships that provide linking ties are crucial elements in the development of learning and capable communities. Yet overreliance on outside forces can also undercut the internal cohesion and confidence of the community itself. The research surveyed in earlier chapters strongly suggests that heterogeneous networks are needed, not instead of but alongside homogeneous ties. Without intervention, networks are likely to reach the limits that are set by the social and cultural boundaries of their members' lifeworlds. The Northern Ireland evidence showed instances where the very real benefits of informal knowledge exchanges are often confined within a particular, bounded network; information and skills that are only available outside that specific network are therefore inaccessible. Moreover, informal knowledge exchange may in some circumstances foster insiderism and cartel-like behaviour; people may exploit their network resources to learn how to avoid regulations and mislead inspectors, or avoid the unwanted attentions of the Drugs Squad. Such self-imposed boundaries to network resources may be highly functional for network members at one level. To take one example, support groups often exclude outsiders in order to maintain a critical perspective among members; however, they can then do little to bring about change because they offered few ties to powerful networks that could provide access to alternative sources of knowledge, skills and ideas (for example, Davis, 2001).

This may be sufficient for some groups who share strongly held norms of opposition to the dominant order. In such cases, a self-excluding network can provide a meaningful source of esteem and emotional support precisely because it helps to maintain a distance from despised ascendant values and contacts. Some of the working-class communities in Northern Ireland appeared to be using their network resources in precisely this way, and the professionals who were working with them often expressed mixed feelings about the consequences. Yet this process of coping by bonding becomes simultaneously a cause of further exclusion. For Portes, who gives the example of Black Americans who attack those of their number who seek to join the (predominantly White) middle class, it represents the imposition of downward levelling norms which then combine with the prejudice and hostility of a discriminatory elite (Portes, 1998, p 15). Yet self-exclusion can also be a sensible strategy, a way of negotiating risks arising from uncertainty and unfamiliarity.

Resolving these issues is no simple matter, nor a rapid one. In their study of the implementation of the Scottish Executive's policies for New Community Schools, Nixon et al (2001, p 348) claim that any successful interprofessional initiative requires the undoing of years of specialist professional socialisation, and argue for periods of interprofessional continuing training as a solution. An official review of university/business collaboration in Britain similarly concluded that many people working in government agencies to promote brokerage and knowledge transfer simply lacked the skills and expertise to do so effectively (Lambert, 2003, p 68). Little systematic evidence exists as to the effectiveness of such interventions, but at this stage interprofessional learning seems the best option available (Zwarenstein et al, 1999).

Heterogeneity is therefore a useful resource, but a risky one. Ties with people like oneself tend to be good at passing on particular types of information or skill, which are important to the entire community. When combined with a high degree of social closure, bonding ties can reinforce dominant values, and minimise threats of dissonant behaviour. They are therefore particularly valuable in socialising young people and, where a community places a high value on school achievement, this will be reflected in the behaviour of the young, as is the case in Northern Ireland. More generally, bonding social capital is good at coping with hard times and tough circumstances. Network resources have been critical in Northern Ireland in enabling people, particularly in working-class neighbourhoods in the cities and in some of the farming communities, to survive and sometimes thrive during the years of conflict. In these circumstances, capabilities for sharing information and skills – and a willingness to deny these to outsiders – were critical metaskills of survival, arising from the strength of people's bonding ties. But they also brought people up against the limits of their lifeworlds.

Community development and local economic regeneration is one field where the concept of social capital seems to offer implications for policy and practice. Active citizenship and volunteering is another, and one of particular relevance for this study given the evidence in Chapter Three on the positive relationship between civic engagement and attitudes towards learning. Likewise, I have already noted the close historical associations between active citizenship and adult education in Europe, Australasia and North America (Bron, 1995). However, I also recognise that the older social movements that promoted this symbiotic relationship are in decline, and the creation of welfare systems has tended to blunt their oppositional edge; moreover, it is highly unlikely that they can be revived simply by an act of will, however sustained. Newer social movements and voluntary organisations are more self-contained educationally than were the classical social movements of the 19th and 20th centuries. Partly, this is because their memberships tend to be drawn disproportionately from the very highly educated, and are able to satisfy many of their own knowledge requirements without the intervention of educational institutions (Field, 2003a, p 75). Partly, it arises from the tendency of newer social movements to "resist the logic of technical objects, instruments of power and social integration" (Touraine, 1995, p 230) so that the processes of setting themselves apart from wider collectivities, including educational institutions, is precisely what defines their autonomy.

What about those who do not take part in civic activity of any kind? The evidence of the net benefits from civic engagement, including the most obvious one of influencing public matters in the direction one favours, is consistent. Chapter Three demonstrated that, in terms of values, those who are most engaged tend to show precisely those attitudes and values – or dispositions – that are associated with a sense of agency, of being able to exert control over key parts of one's life. It follows that people who do not take part are accordingly disenfranchised from those knowledge assets, including the affective capabilities that are vital to a sense of individual and collective efficacy.

Volunteering – including the newer forms of civic engagement – continues to be dominated by the middle classes. Some forms of volunteering may bring middle-class people into contact with others from very different backgrounds, and thereby contribute to overall social solidarity. In essence, this mixing of the classes is what appears to have taken place during the Second World War, albeit not often as a result of volunteering (though it is worth remembering that voluntarism, both formally through the civil defence and similar communal organisations, and informally through mutual aid, did mushroom as a result of wartime conditions), producing what Putnam has called the long civic generation that is now passing away. However, while there is good evidence to show that civic engagement is generally high among the middle classes, it is in decline among the working class, with particularly sharp falls in the membership and activity levels of separate working-class institutions like trades unions, which are in decline (Li et al, 2003). The risk, then, is that in this context, middle-class volunteering is contributing – however unintentionally – towards greater inequality of well-being.

Public support for volunteering promotes a general good, and is therefore desirable in itself. In so far as it brings people together from diverse backgrounds, it provides a space for what Engeström calls expansive learning (Engeström, 2004). In view of these benefits, Peter Alheit has even suggested an obligatory period of service in what he calls the "civil sector", consisting of non-commodified public services (Alheit, 1996). Alheit's proposal, while somewhat sketchy and deliberately provocative, is an interesting one, involving a basic income, vouchers for education and training, and the possibility of spending phases in the civil sector throughout one's working life. The key outcomes, he believes, would include greater "public-spiritedness and communitarianism" and a steep rise in individual demand for education (Alheit, 1996, pp 4-5).

In Britain, most recent policy initiatives have been targeted at young people rather than adults. Examples include the large-scale programme of 'gap year' volunteering developed in Britain, largely focused on university students, which is underscored by explicit references to building social capital (Scottish Executive, 2004). A comparatively small number of policy initiatives has focused on adults, such as the local projects sponsored by the Department for Education and Skills (DfES) in England under its Adult and Community Learning Fund (ACLF) or the Experience Corps that has been encouraged by the Chancellor, Gordon Brown. Part of the success of the ACLF appears to be due to DfES' willingness to hand management of the Fund over to two non-governmental organisations involved in adult learning. The Experience Corps in Britain is modelled on an American initiative that was developed as an independent social enterprise – a programme recruiting older adults to volunteer in underserved elementary schools; its apparent success may again be due to the programme's relative autonomy from state control, since it approaches school boards as an equal partner rather than a servant (Glass et al, 2004). The importance of arm's length approaches to volunteering has been widely noted (Dhesi, 2000).

Fostering civic engagement is likely to require a longer-term approach than is usual in a democratic political cycle. Putnam's study of political institutions in Italy traced the roots of civic disengagement in the South to the legacy of the Norman invasion, which might imply a perspective much too long term for even the most far-sighted policy maker (Putnam, 1993). In his reflections on the process of building an effective civil society in central and eastern Europe, Ralf Dahrendorf thought that at least two generations would be needed of slow, organic change (Dahrendorf, 1990). Misztal notes that "collective goods need to be imagined, debated and agreed upon" (Misztal, 2000, p 126). The formation of positive social capital is, then, both a highly contingent learning process, and one which requires a willingness to take a very long view indeed. This is quite obviously at odds with the dominant culture of policy making in democratic societies, which rarely extends beyond the next election. In politics, one former British Prime Minister, Harold Wilson, asserted, a week is a long time.

Economic policy is a third area of potential intervention, and one that has been of increasing interest to adult educators in recent years. There has been growing debate in the regional development literature about the contribution of networks and proximity to innovation and growth (Maskell et al, 1998; Cooke, 2002; Van Laere and Heene, 2003; Faris, 2004). Putnam's general assertion of the value of civic engagement to economic performance may not at first appear to offer much help to hard-pressed policy makers. It is by no means obvious that the members of civic associations are likely to be key contributors to business growth – for example, if they do, it is unlikely to be extensive. Rather, entrepreneurs are more likely to encounter one another in business contexts, which promote both a flow of information and allow collective lobbying (Cooke, 2002, pp 91-3). However, Philip Cooke also notes that strong local ties can help to underpin expectations that trust and reciprocity will be enforced (Cooke, 2002, p 96). It is also arguable that they can boost confidence in a local area, and thus engender a spirit of optimism and enterprise more generally.

Such ties may be particularly important for those undertakings that have the most limited access to more conventional business assets, such as financial and human capital. Thus the Lambert review of business/university collaboration in the UK concluded that, while even the largest companies often found it easiest to work with local higher education institutions, proximity was particularly important for smaller firms. This was not simply a matter of time and money, but also of cultural bridging; for many who have never attended a university, and even for those who have, academics can appear rather "forbidding" and their language and values are not always easily accessible to outsiders (Lambert, 2003, p 79). For Lambert, the solution lay in the creation of localised clusters of the kind that have already emerged in Silicon Valley in North America or around Cambridge in Britain, backed up by other systematic opportunities for informal and formal interaction between the various levels of the business and academic communities (Lambert, 2003, pp 68-70). As Maskell points out, the investment of time and energy needed to build trust may seem rather too long term for impatient entrepreneurs or even busy academics. As he rather caustically puts it, "Few who have witnessed Scandinavian consensus-seeking processes at close quarters will probably feel tempted to praise their simplicity or effectiveness" (Maskell, 2000, p 120; see Billett and Seddon, 2004, p 64 for an Australian example).

Yet the benefits from such engagement in the longer term are substantial, in so far as negotiation and exploration over time involve learning. In Denmark, for example, fears of losing market share following the introduction of the Single European Market in 1992 persuaded the Ministry of Trade to launch the Danish Network Programme (Cooke, 2002, pp 114-15). Through its agency, the Danish Technological Institute, the government started by trying to win support from leaders of small firms and training network brokers, then moving on to subsidising the building of clusters, each of which involved eight or so small firms plus a research centre. Subsequently, when the government subsidy ran out, many firms chose to continue voluntarily, with long-term consequences. "When imported disruptions necessitate rapid restructuring and unlearning," Maskell suggests, "the necessary framework can already be in place" (Maskell, 2000, p 120).

Much the same can be said for networks and knowledge inside a firm. In a detailed case study of a software engineering company, which they described as a typical 'knowledge-intensive firm', Swart and Kinnie conclude that "an intellectual capital advantage can be gained by ensuring that the processes for managing people provide close support for the processes of knowledge sharing" (Swart and Kinnie, 2003, p 60). In their case study, the company had created an informal process of personnel management based on mentoring and project teams, and asked specialist staff working as project managers to train and develop their team, regardless of each individual's position in the formal hierarchy; new staff were recruited using personal networks rather than open advertisement, with communications skills and creativity forming key criteria for appointment, alongside specialist software knowledge; and knowledge was shared through cross-functional meetings, voluntary membership of working committees, and an actively developed intranet. At organisational level, it has been suggested that transparent procedures and an open culture are critical to network learning, creating receptive capacity and trust (Kekäle and Viitala, 2003, p 246). So, at the very least, this has policy implications for the internal management and organisation of public sector bodies, where such behaviour can be modelled and encouraged.

Finally, there is growing recognition of the importance of new technologies for both sociability and learning. As we have seen, the question of whether online communications promote or hinder sociability is a controversial one. Some see the technology as a new basis for inclusion and cohesion, while others see it as a threat. The pervasive existence of new tools of communication, though, is an established fact. Just how the Internet may be used, and misused, to promote sociability and learning is the subject of a recent doctoral thesis by Sara Ferlander (Ferlander, 2003). Ferlander examines the contrasting effects of two different policy initiatives in a disadvantaged neighbourhood in Stockholm, both of which were aimed at encouraging digital inclusion and building social capital. One, a local net, failed and was abandoned; the second, an internet café, managed to attract large numbers of users who took up informal support and training, acquired valuable IT skills and – according to Ferlander – reported higher levels of friendship, trust and tolerance than non-users (Ferlander, 2003, pp 305-18).

Ferlander's findings are consistent with other studies of online learning that emphasise the significance of combining digital interaction with offline encounters, whether with fellow learners, tutors or other sources of support. Such mixtures of direct and remote interaction may be particularly helpful in promoting online community learning among disadvantaged populations, where levels of Internet access may otherwise be low, and where people's communications skills may not always make for easy use of keyboarding and text-based knowledge. Where such blended learning communities are not practicable, some recommend the development of specific skills and techniques to promote empathy at a distance (Salmon, 2001). This approach has been extended to distance learning programmes by the University of Phoenix, the largest distance education provider in the US, which has a reported completion rate of 65% over seven years. One factor involved is the formal creation of cohort groups: "Whether in online settings or in classroom environments, all instruction takes place in cohort groups of about 15 students. These groups take all-prescribed courses in lock-step fashion and, according to the current chief academic officer, form tight-knit learning communities that result in lifelong friendships" (Barefoot, 2004, p 15).

So, although it is certainly possible to build community through online methods, there is plenty of evidence to suggest that online interaction needs to be accompanied by personal mediation in order to build reciprocity and trust.

If policy makers are to promote adult learning and invest in community building, the evidence summarised in earlier chapters suggests that they should see these goals as closely linked. As the survey evidence in Chapter Three confirms, people who are active in one sphere are usually positive about the other, suggesting that these attitudes and behaviours form a related cluster, or disposition. So, while many people may see both adult learning and sociability as desirable in themselves, if they are closely bound up with one another, then a common set of integrated policy instruments is likely to be mutually reinforcing. Conversely, policy measures that damage learning opportunities will also reduce social interaction; and measures that undermine community will also remove opportunities for learning. Governments that wish to promote active adult learning may therefore want to increase the active membership of all kinds of associations, and take measures that improve people's capacity to pursue leisure opportunities. Both will provide stimuli and tools for learning, and the learning will feed back into the community.

This goal also requires cooperation between people delivering services, even if they work in different departments or organisations. The difficulties of interagency partnership working are well known. As a feminist adult educator wrote some decades ago, reflecting on the experience of developing local learning programmes for women, "professional rivalry is sustained by careful lines of demarcation between providers" (Thompson, 1983, p 186). So powerfully entrenched are professional identities in the public service sector that it has even been suggested that professionals engaged in partnership work are committing "cultural suicide" in that, by consenting to collaborate with others, they are cutting themselves off from their own professional culture (Beattie et al, 1996, p 685). This is a remarkably conservative view, suggesting not only that particular cultural identities are fixed, but that any adaptation or compromise amounts to a tragic deflation on one's identity assets.

Bonding social capital is associated with a pattern of learning that tends to promote stability rather than change, solidity rather than flexibility. Some of the Northern Ireland evidence relates to this type of knowledge exchange, which seems to be very good at enabling people to cope in tough circumstances, without exposing themselves to the risks that might arise from sustained contact with outsiders – including the risks of "cultural suicide". Yet this type of learning is therefore low on precisely those qualities that appear to be central to work and life in disorganised, truly global capitalism. To promote innovation and challenge our existing views and habits, we need connections to people with dissimilar outlooks to our own, living and working in different situations, and drawing on different biographical experiences (Engeström, 2004). These connections give us access to divergent information and skills, and disrupt our habits of thought and deed, sometimes in ways that make us feel uncomfortable.

The practical challenges of promoting both group solidarity and linking ties are considerable ones for community developers. At a policy level, though, they seem to be quite widely accepted, at least within the UK, where they are often tied to ideas about active citizenship and adult learning. Interestingly, much of the UK debate has been taken forward by people working not in the departments responsible for education or social affairs, but elsewhere – in the Home Office, for instance, or the Social Exclusion Unit.

A plea for social literacy[2]

It is a mistake to see lifelong learning as simply another phrase for adult education. A shift towards a learning society requires changes across the formal curriculum – in schools, colleges, universities and training agencies. Critically, this means constant attention to the way in which people learn how to learn – and thereby acquire habits and skills that will either help or hinder them in learning throughout and across the lifespan (Field, 2000, pp 134-41). But in a more fluid, open and separating society, it also means acquiring the skills required to make sense of the changing social structures and relationships that we encounter and create throughout our lives.

Looked at this way, it is clear that much social literacy is acquired informally. People learn how to relate to one another in much the same way as they acquire their native language – by watching, listening, practising and being corrected. It is a good example of what Lave and Wenger (1991) call situated learning, where novices acquire proficiency through legitimate participation on the periphery. Yet, as with so many skills that are learned in this way, there is a risk that the skillset will be limited by the boundaries of the community of practice in which one does most of one's learning. To use the language of social capital, people who acquire their social literacy from their bonding ties will find that they lack critical capabilities – including affective ones such as confidence – when they move beyond the borders of their existing community of practice. This might not have mattered much to people who lived in situations where bonding ties were the only sources of support that mattered, and where outside influences were mediated by other, known individuals. In contemporary societies such constraints are likely to prove damaging, and the support mechanisms may even prove suffocating; where people lack confidence in their capabilities for handling multiple, shifting, heterogeneous ties, they are likely to develop personal strategies leading to withdrawal and avoidance.

Barbara Misztal claims that in contemporary societies such factors as greater mobility, the expanding division of labour (especially, perhaps, for women) and the compression of time-space distances are increasing not just the scale and range of many people's encounters with unknown others. They also introduce a new element of risk, not just in the rather exceptional circumstances of Northern Ireland, for Misztal argues that "every such interaction puts our status under continuous review" and therefore creates sources of possible anxiety and fear (Misztal, 2000, p 146). For Sztompka, these changes mean that "large segments of the contemporary social world have become opaque for their members" (Sztompka, 1999, p 13). Life was at least simpler in a world where status distinctions were visible in people's clothing, their posture, their hairstyle, even the state of their teeth, as well as in the rituals of everyday conversations. The very relaxed and open appearance of fluid social relationships, according to Misztal, add up to a "tyranny of informality" in which "the forced imposition of an artificial equality" may undermine private/public boundaries, inhibit communication and produce a constant examination of the self (Misztal, 2000, p 239). People therefore depend for their well-being and even safety on their ability to "develop increasingly sophisticated skills of reading and interpreting symbols and signs that others exhibit in everyday life" (Misztal, 1996, p 116).

While the impact of these shifts may be uneven, they appear to be affecting all strata and all social groups. Yet this does not mean that different groups are affected equally, for some people are much better placed than others to navigate the new opaque spaces of late modernity. And capacities are also influenced by the political decisions that determine how the state intervenes in these processes. In Britain, Stephen Ball has described the way in which this has helped create "a regime of risk identification which rests primarily upon individual responsibility", combined with a loss of support for egalitarian social and educational policies (Ball, 2003, pp 20-1). I would therefore argue strongly for investment in social literacy, not only for young people but also for adults, including older adults for whom much of the new social etiquette feels like a mystery *and* a threat.

Some people, of course, assume that social capabilities are innate. Either people are born with these attributes, or they are taught by your parents while you are small. Or the qualities needed for cooperation are bred through the school of tough knocks: workers learn solidarity by experiencing exploitation, lovers learn sensitivity by facing rejection, aircrews learn teamwork through having vigorous arguments about what to do next.... The result of leaving it to the marketplace and experience is that such skills are unequally distributed, and this therefore reinforces other inequalities – indeed, more than reinforcing them, it may also help to legitimate them, because inequalities of wealth, status and power are seen to be 'fair', because they are the product of an inability to get on with others and contribute to the wider community.

Equity and inclusion are one side of the coin. Economically, these are also skills that have a growing value in the labour market. If it is true that employers increasingly find that job applicants lack 'soft skills', as is often claimed, then this is almost certainly because of changes in the economy rather than a decline in sociability among young people (Scottish Enterprise, 2003). In Britain, the main growth in employment has taken place within the service sector – where people frequently need to interact with customers and other employees in order to deliver a product. Even those who have relatively few formal credentials, and are entering jobs where the formal skills requirements are minimal, may well need quite advanced 'soft skills'; examples include bar workers, bouncers and waiters. Across most sectors there is also continuing growth in professional and associate professional occupations, most of which again require 'soft skills'. So, a curriculum for social literacy is potentially beneficial not only in respect of everyday social encounters, but also within many different types of work.

What would a curriculum for social literacy cover? This question is easier to ask than to answer – though simple answers always command a ready market at times of flux. Ideas such as 'emotional intelligence' have taken root with a speed that goes far beyond their intellectual merits. Particularly important here is the idea that emotional intelligence is something that can be learned, a set of competences that can be gained – usually, it seems, by professionals and managers – through a mixture of training and self-regulation (Fineman, 2000, pp 104-5). However, while emotional competences may be valuable, particularly in enhancing communicative capacities, they are traded by trainers as essentially individual skills, underpinned by some rather suspect theories of human intelligence. The question here is whether we can identify broad sets of skills that enable people to read relationships in ways that help them solve problems and cooperate effectively with others.

Recent debates over key competences – or *compétences clefs*, *Schlusselqualifikationen* – seem to have reached a general consensus on the desirability of social capabilities. One meeting of education ministers from the OECD member states concluded confidently that "our goal is competencies for all – basic competencies on which other learning depends, and the high-level intellectual and social competencies on which full engagement in the knowledge society depends" (OECD, 2001b, p 3).

However, they also confessed that "it is not easy to identify with sufficient certainty the new competencies needed" (OECD, 2001b, p 3). Yet definitions are emerging, if hestitantly. In broad terms, Asaf Darr (2004, p 57) suggests: "Social skills include interactive skills and strategic planning involved in constructing and manipulating a network of social ties". Eva Cox has defined social competence as the skills required for "making and retaining relationships, developing networks for use and pleasure, or a capacity to read social mores so as to feel integrated into one's social milieu" (Cox, 2000, p 1).

There is already abundant evidence of learning producing new social capital resources (Schuller et al, 2004). This includes the acquisition by individuals of new cognitive and affective skills, such as confidence and self-esteem. Moreover, learning appears to compensate at least partly for socioeconomic disadvantage in these respects. Survey data for England indicate that unemployed people and benefit dependants who undertook taught learning were markedly more likely to identify increases in both confidence and self-esteem as a result of their course than were other respondents (Fitzgerald et al, 2003, p 77). Of course, such growing sense of self can be empowering, and this in turn can be a cause of conflict, certainly within families and possibly also within wider sets of relationships such as local communities (Hammond, 2004, pp 47-8).

Nor is this evidence confined to formal education in institutions. Volunteering itself produces new demands for skills and knowledge that can be acquired informally. In her ongoing study of informal learning in voluntary organisations in Britain and Finland, Marion Fields found that, while Finns tended to emphasise the acquisition of administrative skills (meeting management, financial administration, and so on), Britons were more likely to mention communicative and other personal skills; however, this was a difference of emphasis rather an absolute gulf, with both sets of respondents mentioning similar sets of skills (Fields, 2003).

Opening up the debate

This book has emphasised the role of social capital in creating as well as exchanging knowledge, and the role of learning in building social capital. This pattern appears to be a highly significant one, which is characteristic of our actually existing learning society – that is, the learning society in which we presently live, rather than the utopian (or dystopian) one of the future. Its hallmarks are that new knowledge is created all the time, and is instantly applicable, as a kind of "doing knowledge" that "determines the structures of society far beyond the purely occupational domain and lends them a dynamic of ever-shorter cycles" (Alheit and Dausein, 2002, p 8). Rather than the simple transfer of fixed bodies of codified and abstracted knowledge, education and training are increasingly embedded in wider, interactive processes of societal "knowledge osmosis" (Alheit and Dausein, 2002, p 8), a continuous exchange of individual and collective knowledge production and ever more systematised knowledge management.

Yet for the past three decades, much policy debate on education and training has focused on an ever more narrow and impoverished view of learning. Underpinning the policy thinking has been a largely instrumental view of the purposes of learning, whether couched in terms of qualifications that enable further progression and transition inside the formal education and training system, or job-related skills that will promote employability and enhance individuals' careers. All too often, ideas of a wider purpose to learning start and end either with individual self-fulfilment or national economic growth. Ideas of 'performativity' appeal to many people because they concentrate on what people can do as a result of learning: successful learning experiences enable people to perform in tests, acquire qualifications, get jobs and seek promotion. But there is more to learning than this. As well as achieving instrumental aims and objectives, and promoting particular abilities and knowledge, "the deeper significance of learning lies through its forming of our powers and capacities, in our unfolding agency", enabling us "to develop our distinctive agency as a human being" (Nixon et al, 1996, p 49).

The model of learning used in this volume is an inherently social one. Some years ago, Michael Young distinguished three dominant versions of the learning society: the 'schooling model', with people being recruited en masse to existing providers; the 'credential model', where formal certificated qualifications offer a threshold to further certificated qualifications; and the 'access model', which involves transforming providers to make them more learner (or customer) focused (Young, 1998). Against these, Young proposed the alternative of what he called a 'connective model', in which education and training providers were required to negotiate the terms of partnerships and establish common goals together with other collective actors in the public, private and voluntary sectors. While avoiding the supply-driven rigidities of the 'schooling model' and the market inequities and turbulence of the 'access model', the 'connective model' does carry risks, as any partnership tends over time to be dominated by a small number of insiders, who then use it as a vehicle for pursuing their own interests. Nevertheless, it offers us the best way of building bridges between the worlds of formal and informal learning, and of ensuring that the fragmented and distributed experiences of adults' various learning episodes are connected and acknowledged in a responsive curriculum. It also offers a realistic means of bringing knowledge and application into constant interaction.

Such arguments may seem hopelessly optimistic. Even in a prosperous, democratic and open society, it might seem naïve to call for policies and practices that will build trust and reciprocity, and help people to reconstruct forms of community that are appropriate to a reflexive, networked world. Is it not self-evident that we live in a fast-moving world, where few individuals can afford the luxury of spending time to really know workmates and neighbours, who may themselves move on at any time? The central logic of this book runs completely counter to any such pessimism.

Notes

[1] Between 1997 and 2000, I served on the National Advisory Group for Continuing Education and Lifelong Learning, which was chaired by Bob Fryer, and whose report influenced the government's Green Paper on lifelong learning (Fryer, 1998; DfEE, 1998).

[2] I realise that some readers will have direct experience of academics' social skills, and may be mightily entertained by the idea of an academic speaking in favour of social literacy.

References

Aldridge, F. and Tuckett, A. (2003) *A sharp reverse: NIACE survey on adult participation*, Leicester: National Institute of Adult Continuing Education.

Alheit, P. (1994) *Zivile Kultur. Verlust und Wideraneignung der Moderne*, Frankfurt-am-Main: Campus Verlag.

Alheit, P. (1996) 'A provocative proposal: "from labour society to learning society"', *Lifelong Learning in Europe*, vol 2, pp 3-5.

Alheit, P. and Dausein, B. (2002) 'The "double face" of lifelong learning: two analytical perspectives on a "silent revolution"', *Studies in the Education of Adults*, vol 34, no 1, pp 2-22.

Avis, J. (2004) 'Re-thinking trust in a performative culture: the case of post-compulsory education', in J. Satterthwaite, E. Atkinson and W. Martin (eds) *The disciplining of education: New languages of power and resistance*, Stoke-on-Trent: Trentham Books, pp 69-88.

Ball, S. (1993) *Class strategies and the education market: The middle class and social advantage*, London: RoutledgeFalmer.

Ball, S. (2003) *Class strategies and the education market: The middle class and social advantage*, London: RoutledgeFalmer.

Barefoot, B. (2004) 'Higher education's revolving door: confronting the problem of student drop out in US colleges and universities', *Open Learning*, vol 19, no 1, pp 9-18.

Barz, H. (2002) *Weiterbildung und soziale Milieus*, Neuwied: Luchterhand Verlag.

Barz, H. and Tippelt, R. (1998) 'The influence of social milieus on attitudes and activities of women in lifelong learning', in P. Alheit and E. Kammler (eds) *Lifelong learning and its impact on social and regional development*, Bremen: Donat Verlag, pp 527-46.

Beattie, J., Cheek, J. and Gibson, T. (1996) 'The politics of collaboration as viewed through the lens of a collaborative nursing research project', *Journal of Advanced Nursing*, vol 24, pp 682-7.

Beck, U. (1992) *Risk society*, London: Sage Publications.

Beck, U. (2000) 'Living your own life in a runaway world: individualisation, globalisation and politics', in W. Hutton and A. Giddens (eds) *On the edge: Living with global capitalism*, London: Jonathan Cape, pp 164-74.

Becker, G.S. (1964) *Human capital: A theoretical and empirical analysis*, New York, NY: National Bureau of Economic Research.

Benn, R. (1996) 'Access for adults to higher education: targeting or self-selection?', *Journal of Access Studies*, vol 11, no 2, pp 165-76.

Benn, R. (2000) 'The genesis of active citizenship in the learning society', *Studies in the Education of Adults*, vol 32, no 2, pp 241-56.

Billett, S. and Seddon, T. (2004) 'Building community through social partnerships and vocational education and training', *Journal of Vocational Education and Training*, vol 56, no 1, pp 51-67.

Black, B. (2004) 'The changing world of work', in K. Lloyd, P. Devine, A.M. Gray and D. Heenan (eds) *Social attitudes in Northern Ireland: The ninth report*, London: Pluto, pp 67-80.

Blaxter, L. and Hughes, C. (2001) 'Social capital: a critique', in J. Thompson (ed) *Stretching the academy: The politics and practice of widening participation in higher education*, Leicester: National Institute for Adult Continuing Education.

Boon, M. and Curtice, J. (2003) *Scottish elections research, May-June 2003*, London: ICM.

Boreham, N. (2002) 'Work process knowledge in technological and organizational development', in N. Boreham, R. Samurçay and M. Fischer (eds) *Work process knowledge*, London: Routledge, pp 1-14.

Boreham, N. (2004) 'A theory of collective competence: challenging the neo-liberal individualisation of performance at work', *British Journal of Educational Studies*, vol 52, no 1, pp 5-17.

Bourdieu, P. (1977) 'Cultural reproduction and social reproduction', in J. Karabel and A.H. Halsey (eds) *Power and ideology in education*, New York, NY: Oxford University Press, pp 487-511.

Bourdieu, P. (1980) 'Le capital social: notes provisoires', *Actes de la récherche en sciences sociales*, pp 2-3.

Bourdieu, P. (1984) *Distinction: A social critique of the judgement of taste*, London: Routledge.

Bourdieu, P. (1986) 'The forms of capital', in J.G. Richardson (ed) *Handbook of theory and research for the sociology of education*, New York, NY: Greenwood Press, pp 241-58.

Bourdieu, P. (1988) *Homo academicus*, Cambridge: Polity Press.

Bourdieu, P. and Wacquant, L. (1992) *An invitation to reflexive sociology*, Chicago, IL: University of Chicago Press.

Boyne, R. (2002) 'Bourdieu: from class to culture', *Theory, Culture & Society*, vol 19, no 3, pp 117-28.

Brandstetter, G. and Kellner, W. (2001) (eds) *Frewilliges Engagement und Erwachsenenbildung. Wege der Identifikation und Bewertung des informellen Lernens*, Vienna: Ring Österreichischer Bildungswerke.

Braun, S. (2002) 'Soziales Kapital, sozialer Zusammenheit und soziale Ungleichheit', *Aus Politik und Zeitgeschichte*, vol 29-30, pp 6-12.

Bron, A. (1995) 'Adult education and civil society in a comparative and historical perspective', in M. Bron and M. Malewski (eds) *Adult education and democratic citizenship*, Wroctaw: Wydawnictwo Uniwersytetu Wroctawskiego, pp 15-26.

Burn, G. (2003) *The north of England home service*, London: Faber and Faber.

Bynner, J. and Hammond, C. (2004) 'The benefits of adult learning: quantitative insights', in T. Schuller, J. Preston, C. Hammond, A. Brassett-Grundy and J. Bynner (eds) *The benefits of learning: The impact of education on health, family life and social capital*, London: RoutledgeFalmer, pp 161-78.

Castells, M. (1996) *The information age, volume 1: The rise of the network society*, Oxford: Basil Blackwell.

Causer, D. and Virdee, P. (eds) (2004) *Regional trends 38*, London: The Stationery Office.

CEC (Commission of the European Communities) (1994) *Competitiveness, employment, growth*, Luxembourg: Office for Official Publications.

CEC (2000) *A memorandum on lifelong learning*, Brussels: CEC.

CEC (2003) *Building the knowledge society: Social and human capital interactions*, Brussels: CEC.

CEC (2004) *EUROSTAT Yearbook 2004: The statistical guide to Europe: Data 1992-2002*, Luxembourg: Office for Official Publications of the European Union.

Church, J. (ed) (1996) *Regional trends 31*, London: The Stationery Office.

CIPD (Chartered Institute of Personnel and Development) (2003) *Reorganising for success: CEOs' and HR managers' perceptions*, London: CIPD.

Cloonan, M. (2004) 'A capital project? The "New Deal for musicians" in Scotland', *Studies in the Education of Adults*, vol 36, no 1, pp 40-56.

Coare, P. and Johnston, R. (eds) (2003) *Adult learning, citizenship and community voices: Exploring community-based practice*, Leicester: National Institute of Adult Continuing Education.

Cochinaux, P. and de Woot, P. (1995) *Moving towards a learning society*, Geneva/Brussels: Conseil des Recteurs d'Europe/European Round Table of Industrialists.

Coleman, J.S. (1988-89) 'Social capital in the creation of human capital', *American Journal of Sociology*, vol 94, pp 95-120.

Coleman, J.S. (1994) *Foundations of social theory*, Cambridge, MA: Belknap Press.

Coleman, J.S. and Hoffer, T. (1987) *Public and private schools: The impact of communities*, New York, NY: Basic Books.

Coleman, J.S., Hoffer, T. and Kilgore, S. (1982) *High school achievement: Public, Catholic and private schools compared*, New York, NY: Basic Books.

Coleman, J.S., Campbell, E.Q., Hobson, C.J., McPartland, J., Mood, A.M., Weinfeld, F.D. and York, R.L. (1966) *Equality of educational opportunity*, Washington, DC: United States Government Printing Office.

Colley, H. (2003) *Mentoring for social inclusion*, London: RoutledgeFalmer.

Colley, H., Hodkinson, P. and Malcolm, J. (2003) *Informality and formality in learning: A report for the Learning and Skills Research Centre*, London: Learning and Skills Development Agency.

Cooke, P. (2002) *Knowledge economies: Clusters, learning and cooperative advantage*, London: Routledge.

Cox, E. (2000) 'Learning social literacy', *Adult Learning Commentary*, vol 15, 21 June 2000, accessed on 13 July 2004 at www.ala.asn.au/commentaries/Cox2106.pdf

Cross, K.P. (1981) *Adults as learners*, San Francisco, CA: Jossey-Bass.

Crowther, J. (2004) '"In and against" lifelong learning: flexibility and the corrosion of character', *International Journal of Lifelong Education*, vol 23, no 2, pp 125-36.

Dahrendorf, R. (1990) *Reflections on the evolution in Europe*, London: Chatto and Windus.

Dakhli, M. and de Clercq, D. (2004) 'Human capital, social capital and innovation: a multi country study', *Entrepreneurship & Regional Development*, vol 16, pp 107-28.

Daly, M. (2004) 'Family relations and social networks in Northern Ireland', in K. Lloyd, P. Devine, A.M. Gray and D. Heenan (eds) *Social attitudes in Northern Ireland: The ninth report*, London: Pluto, pp 53-66.

Darr, A. (2004) 'The interdependence of social and technical skills in the sale of emergent technology', in C. Warhurst, I. Gregulis and E. Keep (eds) *The skills that matter*, London: Palgrave, pp 55-71.

Dasgupta, P. (2000) 'Economic progress and the idea of social capital', in P. Dasgupta and I. Serageldin (eds) *Social capital: A multifaceted perspective*, Washington, DC: World Bank, pp 325-424.

Davis, K.S. (2001) '"Peripheral and subversive": women making connections and challenging the boundaries of the science community', *Science Education*, vol 85, no 4, pp 368-409.

Dearden, C. and Becker, S. (1998) *Young carers in the UK*, London: Carers National Association.

DfEE (Department for Education and Employment) (1998) *The Learning Age: A renaissance for a new Britain*, Sheffield: DfEE.

Dhesi, A.S. (2000) 'Social capital and community development', *Community Development Journal*, vol 35, no 3, pp 199-214.

Durkheim, E. (1933) *The division of labor in society*, translated by G. Simpson, New York, NY: The Free Press.

Dykstra, P.A. (2004) 'Diversity in partnership histories: implications for older adults' social integration', in C. Phillipson, G. Allan and D. Morgan (eds) *Social networks and social exclusion: Sociological and policy perspectives*, Aldershot: Ashgate, pp 117-41.

EYPRU (Education and Young People Research Unit) (2002) *Programme for international student assessment: Scottish report*, Edinburgh: Scottish Executive Education Department.

Edwards, R., Ranson, S. and Strain, M. (2002) 'Reflexivity: towards a theory of lifelong learning', *International Journal of Lifelong Education*, vol 21, no 6, pp 525-36.

Edwards, R., Nicoll, K., Solomon, N. and Usher, R. (2004) *Rhetoric and educational discourse: Persuasive texts?*, London: RoutledgeFalmer.

Egerton, M. (2002) 'Higher education and civic engagement', *British Journal of Sociology*, vol 53, no 4, pp 603-20.

Elsdon, K.T., Reynolds, J. and Stewart, S. (1995) *Voluntary organisations: Citizenship, learning and change*, Leicester: National Institute of Adult Continuing Education.

Emler, N. and McNamara, S. (1996) 'The social contact patterns of young people: effects of participation in the social institutions of family, education and work', in H. Helve and J. Bynner (eds) *Youth and life management: Research perspectives*, Helsinki: Yliopistopaino, pp 121-39.

Engeström, Y. (2004) 'New forms of learning in co-configuration work', *Journal of Workplace Learning*, vol 16, no 1-2, pp 11-21.

Etzioni, A. (1995) *New communitarian thinking: Persons, virtues, institutions, and communities*, Charlottesville, VA: University Press of Virginia.

European Commission Directorate-General for Research (2002) *Focusing and integrating community research: Citizens and governance in a knowledge-based society. Work programme 2002-2003*, Luxembourg: Office for Official Publications.

European Council of Ministers (2002) *Council Document 5828/02*, accessed on 14 January 2005 at www.register.consilium.eu.int/pdf/en/02/st05/05828en2.pdf

Expert Group on Future Skills Needs (2003) *Fourth report*, Dublin: Forfás.

Faris, R. (2004) *Lifelong learning, social capital and place management in learning communities and regions: A Rubic's cube or a kaleidoscope?*, Melbourne/Stirling: Observatory PASCAL, accessed on 12 September 2004 at www.obs-pascal.com/reports/2004/Faris.html

Ferlander, S. (2003) 'The Internet, social capital and local community', PhD thesis, Stirling: University of Stirling.

Field, J. (1991) 'Social movements: the cutting edge of European adult education?', *International Journal of University Adult Education*, vol 30, no 1, pp 1-11.

Field, J. (1997) 'Northern Ireland', in N. Sargant et al, *The learning divide: A study of participation in adult learning in the United Kingdom*, Leicester: NIACE/DfEE, pp 91-8.

Field, J. (2000) *Lifelong learning and the new educational order*, Stoke on Trent: Trentham.

Field, J. (2003a) *Social capital*, London: Routledge.

Field, J. (2003b) 'Social capital and lifelong learning: survey findings on the relationship between sociability and participation', in N. Sargant and F. Aldridge (eds) *Adult learning and social division: A persistent pattern, vol 2*, Leicester: National Institute of Adult Continuing Education, pp 32-41.

Field, J. (2004) 'Articulation and credit transfer in Scotland: taking the academic highroad or a sideways step in a ghetto?', *Journal of Access Policy & Practice*, vol 1, no 2, pp 85-99.

Field, J. and Schuller, T. (2000) 'Networks, norms and trust: explaining patterns of lifelong learning in Scotland and Northern Ireland', in F. Coffield (ed) *Differing visions of a learning society, vol 2*, Bristol: The Policy Press, pp 95-118.

Fieldhouse, R. (ed) (1996) *A history of modern British adult education*, Leicester: National Institute for Adult Continuing Education.

Fields, M. (2003) *Lifelong learning in voluntary organisations and civil society – work in progress*, Doctoral Summer School, Roskilde University Centre, accessed on 31 May 2004 at www.ruc.dk/inst10/forskerskolen/summerschool2003/index/papers/Marion.doc

Fine, B. (2000) *Social capital versus social theory: political economy and social science at the turn of the millennium*, London: Routledge.

Fineman, S. (2000) 'Commodifying the emotionally intelligent', in S. Fineman (ed) *Emotion in organizations*, London: Sage Publications, pp 101-14.

Fitzgerald, R., Taylor, R. and LaValle, I. (2003) *National adult learning survey 2002*, Sheffield: Department for Education and Skills.

Fordham, P., Poulton, G. and Randle, L. (1979) *Learning networks in adult education: Non-formal education on a housing estate*, London: Routledge and Kegan Paul.

Fox, J. (1997) 'The World Bank and social capital: contesting the concept in practice', *Journal of International Development*, vol 9, no 7, pp 963-71.

Fryer, R.H. (1998) *Learning for the twenty-first century: First report of the National Advisory Group for Continuing Education and Lifelong Learning*, Sheffield: Department for Education and Employment.

Fukuyama, F. (1995) *Trust: The social virtues and the creation of prosperity*, Hamish Hamilton, London.

Gibbon, M., Limoges, C., Nowotny, H., Schwartzman, S., Scott, P. and Trow, M. (1994) *The new production of knowledge*, London: Sage Publications.

Giddens, A. (1984) *The constitution of society*, Cambridge: Polity.

Giddens, A. (1991) *Modernity and self-identity: Self and the society in the late modern age*, Cambridge: Polity.

Giddens, A. (1992) *The transformation of intimacy: sexuality, love and eroticism in modern societies*, Cambridge: Polity.

Glass, T.A., Freedman, M., Carlson, M.C., Hill, J., Frick, K.D., Ialongo, N., McGill, S., Rebok, G.W., Seeman, T., Tielsch, J.M., Wasik, B.A., Zeger, Scott, and Fried, L.P. (2004) 'Experience corps: design of an intergenerational program to boost social capital and promote the health of an aging society', *Journal of Urban Health*, vol 81, no 1, pp 94-105.

Goldman, L. (1995) *Dons and workers: Oxford and adult education since 1850*, Oxford: Oxford University Press.

Gorard, S. and Rees, G. (2002) *Creating a learning society? Learning careers and policies for lifelong learning*, Bristol: The Policy Press.

Gorman, J. (1986) *Banner bright: An illustrated history of trade union banners*, Buckhurst Hill: Scorpion.

Granovetter, M. (1973) 'The strength of weak ties', *American Journal of Sociology*, vol 78, no 4, pp 1350-80.

Groombridge, B., Durant, J., Hampton, W., Woodcock, G. and Wright, A. (1982) *Adult education and participation*, Sheffield: Universities' Council for Adult and Continuing Education.

Hall, P. (1999) 'Social capital in Britain', *British Journal of Political Science*, vol 29, no 3, pp 417-61.

Halman, L. (2001) *The European Values Study: A third wave*, Tilburg: Tilburg University, Netherlands.

Hammond, C. (2004) 'The impacts of learning on well-being, mental health and effective coping', in T. Schuller, J. Preston, C. Hammond, A. Brassett-Grundy and J. Bynner (eds) *The benefits of learning: The impact of education on health, family life and social capital*, London: RoutledgeFalmer, pp 37-56.

Harrison, R. (ed) (1978) *Independent collier: The coal miners as archetypal proletarian reconsidered*, Hassocks: Harvester.

Hedoux, C. (1982) 'Des publics et des non-publics de la formation d'adults', *Revue française de sociologie*, vol 23, pp 253-74.

Heenan, D. (2002) '"It won't change the world but it turned my life around": participants' views on the Personal Adviser Scheme in the New Deal for Disabled People', *Disability & Society*, vol 17, no 4, pp 383-402.

HESA (Higher Education Statistics Agency) (2003) *Higher education management statistics, 2001/02*, Cheltenham: HESA.

Hibbitt, K., Jones, P. and Meegan, R. (2001) 'Tackling social exclusion: the role of social capital in urban regeneration on Merseyside: from mistrust to trust?', *European Planning Studies*, vol 9, no 2, pp 141-61.

Illich, I. (1971) *Deschooling society*, London: Harper and Row.

Jamieson, L. (1998) *Intimacy: Personal relationships in modern societies*, Cambridge: Polity.

Jarvie, G. (2003) 'Communitarianism, sport and social capital: "Neighbourly insights into Scottish sport"', *International Review for the Sociology of Sport*, vol 38, no 2, pp 139-53.

Jarvis, P. (1987) *Adult learning in the social context*, Beckenham: Croom Helm.

Jenkins, R. (1992) *Pierre Bourdieu*, London: Routledge.

Johnston, I. (2002) 'Programme for international student assessment: NI and international results compared', *Labour Market Bulletin*, vol 16, pp 155-66.

Kade, J. and Seitter, W. (1998) 'Bildung-risiko-genuß: Dimensionen und Ambivalenzen lebenslangen Lernens in der Moderne', in R. Brödel (ed) *Lebenslanges Lernen – lebensbegleitende Bildung*, Neuwied: Luchterhand, pp 51-9.

Kekäle, T. and Viitala, R. (2003) 'Do networks learn?', *Journal of Workplace Learning*, vol 15, no 6, pp 245-7.

Kirchhöfer, D. (2000) *Informelles Lernen in alltäglichen Lebensführungen. Chance für berufliche Kompetenzentwicklung*, Qualifikations-Entwicklung-Management, Report 66, Berlin.

Lall, S. (2000) 'Technological change and industrialization in the Asian newly industrializing economies: achievements and challenges', in L. Kim and R.R. Nelson (eds) *Technology, learning and innovation: Experiences of newly industrializing economies*, Cambridge: Cambridge University Press, pp 13-68.

Lambert, R. (2003) *Lambert review of business–university collaboration: Final report*, London: HM Treasury.

Lave, J. and Wenger, E. (1991) *Situated learning*, Cambridge: Cambridge University Press.

Li, Y., Savage, M. and Pickles, A. (2003) 'Social capital and social exclusion in England and Wales (1972-1999)', *British Journal of Sociology*, vol 54, no 4, pp 497-526.

Livingstone, D.W. and Sawchuk, P.H. (2004) *Hidden knowledge: Organized labour in the information age*, Aurora, Ontario: Garamond.

Lovett, T. (1975) *Adult education, community development and the working class*, London: Ward Lock.

Lowndes, V. (2004) 'Getting on or getting by? Women, social capital and political participation', *British Journal of Politics and International Relations*, vol 6, no 1, pp 45-64.

Lundvall, B.-Å. and Johnson, B. (1994) 'The learning economy', *Journal of Industry Studies*, vol 1, no 2, pp 23-42.

McClenaghan, P. (2000) 'Social capital: exploring the theoretical foundations of community development education', *British Educational Research Journal*, vol 26, no 5, pp 565-82.

McGivney, V. (1991) *Education's for other people*, Leicester: National Institute for Adult Continuing Education.

Maloney, W., Smith, G. and Stoker, G. (2000a) 'Social capital and associational life', in S. Baron, J. Field, and T. Schuller (eds) *Social capital: Critical perspectives*, Oxford: Oxford University Press, pp 212-25.

Maloney, W., Smith, G. and Stoker, G. (2000b) 'Social capital and urban governance: adding a more contextualised "top-down" perspective', *Political Studies*, vol 48, no 4, pp 802-20.

Maskell, P. (2000) 'Social capital, innovation and competitiveness', in S. Baron, J. Field and T. Schuller (eds) *Social capital: Critical perspectives*, Oxford: Oxford University Press, pp 111-23.

Maskell, P., Eskelinen, H., Hannibalsson, I., Malmberg, A. and Vatne, E. (1998) *Competitiveness, localized learning and regional development: Specialisation and prosperity in small open economies*, London: Routledge.

Maybe, C., Salaman, G. and Storey, J. (1998) *Human resource management: A strategic introduction*, Oxford, Blackwell.

Merrill, B. (1999) *Gender, change and identity: Mature women students in universities*, Aldershot: Ashgate.

Misztal, B.A. (1996) *Trust in modern societies: The search for the bases of social order*, Cambridge: Polity.

Misztal, B.A. (2000) *Informality: Social theory and contemporary practice*, London: Routledge.

Morgan, S.L. (2000) 'Social capital, capital goods, and the production of learning', *Journal of Socio-Economics*, vol 29, pp 591-5.

Morrissey, M. and McGinn, P. (2001) *Evaluating community based and voluntary activity in Northern Ireland: Interim report*, Belfast: Community Evaluation Northern Ireland.

Morrow, V. (1999) 'Conceptualising social capital in relation to the well-being of children and young people: a critical review,' *Sociological Review*, pp 744-65.

Mouqué, D. (1999) *Sixth periodic report on the social and economic situation and development of the regions of the European Union*, Luxembourg: Office for Official Publications of the European Union.

Murtagh, B. (2002) *Social activity and interaction in Northern Ireland*, Northern Ireland Life and Times Survey Research Update 10, Belfast: ARK.
NESF (National Economic and Social Forum) (2003) *The policy implications of social capital*, Dublin: NESF.
NIAE (National Institute of Adult Education) (1970) *Adult education: Adequacy of provision*, Leicester: NIAE.
NISRA (Northern Ireland Statistics and Research Agency) (2002) *Northern Ireland Census 2001: Key statistics*, Belfast: NISRA.
Nixon, J., Allan, J. and Mannion, G. (2001) 'Educational renewal as a democratic practice: "new' community schooling in Scotland", *International Journal of Inclusive Education*, vol 5, no 4, pp 329-52.
Nixon, J., Martin, J., McKeown, P. and Ranson, S. (1996) *Encouraging learning: Towards a theory of the learning school*, Buckingham: Open University Press.
O'Connell, P.J. (1999) *Adults in training: An international comparison of continuing education and training*, Paris: OECD.
OECD (Organisation for Economic Co-operation and Development) (1996) *Technology, productivity and job creation: Best policy practices*, Paris: OECD.
OECD (2000) *Sustained economic growth and well-being*, Paris: OECD.
OECD (2001a) *The well-being of nations: The role of human and social capital*, Paris: OECD.
OECD (2001b) 'Meeting of the OECD education ministries, Investing in competencies for all. Communiqué', Paris, 3-4 April, Paris: OECD.
PIU (Performance and Innovation Unit) (2002) *Social capital: A discussion paper*, London: Cabinet Office.
Polanyi, M. (1966) *The tacit dimension*, London, Routledge and Kegan Paul.
Porter, M. (1990) *The competitive advantage of nations*, New York, NY: Free Press.
Portes, A. (1998) 'Social capital: its origins and applications in modern sociology', *Annual Review of Sociology*, vol 24, pp 1-24.
Preston, J. (2003) 'Enrolling alone? Lifelong learning and social capital in England', *International Journal of Lifelong Education*, vol 22, no 3, pp 235-48.
Putnam, R.D. (1993) *Making democracy work: Civic traditions in modern Italy*, Princeton, NJ: Princeton University Press.
Putnam, R.D. (1995) 'Bowling alone: America's declining social capital', *Journal of Democracy*, vol 6, pp 65-78.
Putnam, R.D. (2000) *Bowling alone: The collapse and revival of American community*, New York, NY: Simon and Schuster.

Research Forum (2000) *National marketing strategy for skills and lifelong learning: Market segmentation report*, Brisbane: Australian National Training Authority.

Rhodes, R.A.W. (1996) 'The new governance: governing without government', *Political Studies*, vol 44, no 4, pp 652-67.

Robbins, D. (2000) *Bourdieu and culture*, London: Sage Publications.

Roberts, S. (ed) (2003) *A ministry of enthusiasm: Centenary essays on the Workers' Educational Association*, London: Pluto Press.

Robinson, K. (2001) *Out of our minds: Learning to be creative*, Oxford: Capstone.

Rose, J. (2002) *The intellectual life of the British working classes*, New Haven, CT: Yale University Press,.

Rubenson, K. (2001) 'The power of the state: connecting lifelong learning policy and educational practice', in R.M. Cervero and A.L. Wilson (eds) *Power in practice: Adult education and the struggle for knowledge and power in society*, San Francisco, CA: Jossey-Bass, pp 83-104.

Salmon, G. (2001) 'Far from remote', *People Management*, 27 September, pp 34-6.

Salmon, H. (2002) 'Social capital and neighbourhood renewal', *Renewal*, vol 10, no 2, pp 49-55.

Sargant, N. with Field, J., Francis, H., Schuller, T. and Tuckett, A. (1997) *The learning divide: A report of the findings of a UK-wide survey on adult participation in education and learning*, Leicester: National Institute of Adult Continuing Education.

Savage, M., Bagnall, G. and Longhurst, B. (2005) 'Local habitus and working-class culture', in F. Devine, M. Savage, J. Scott and R. Crompton (eds) *Rethinking class: Culture, identities and lifestyle*, Basingstoke, Palgrave Macmillan, pp 95-122.

Schemmann, M. (2002) 'Reflexive modernisation in adult education research: the example of Anthony Giddens' theoretical approach', in A. Bron and M. Schemmann (eds) *Social science theories in adult education research*, Münster: Lit Verlag, pp 64-80.

Schemmann, M. and Bron, M. (eds) (2001) *Adult education and democratic citizenship IV*, Kraków: Impuls.

Schemmann, M. and Reinecke, M. (2002) *Gewerkschaftliche Bildungsarbeit in gesellschaftlichen Wandel*, Kraków: Impuls.

Schinkel, W. (2003) 'Pierre Bourdieu's political turn?', *Theory, Culture and Society*, vol 20, no 6, pp 69-93.

Schuller, T. (2004) 'Studying benefits', in T. Schuller, J. Preston, C. Hammond, A. Brassett-Grundy and J. Bynner (eds) *The benefits of learning: The impact of education on health, family life and social capital*, London: RoutledgeFalmer, pp 3-11.

Schuller, T. and Field, J. (1998) 'Social capital, human capital and the learning society', *International Journal of Lifelong Education*, vol 17, no 4, pp 226-35.

Schuller, T., Baron, S. and Field, J. (2000) 'Social capital: a review and critique', in S. Baron, J. Field and T. Schuller (eds) *Social capital: Critical perspectives*, Oxford: Oxford University Press, pp 1-38.

Schuller, T., Preston, J., Hammond, C., Brassett-Grundy, A. and Bynner, J. (2004) *The benefits of learning: The impact of education on health, family life and social capital*, London: Routledge Falmer.

Scottish Enterprise (2003) *Futureskills Scotland: The Scottish labour market 2003*, Glasgow/Inverness: Scottish Enterprise/Highlands and Islands Enterprise.

Scottish Executive (2003) *Working and learning together to build stronger communities: Community learning and development – working draft guidance*, Edinburgh: Scottish Executive.

Scottish Executive (2004) *Volunteering strategy*, Edinburgh: Scottish Executive.

Seaman, P. and Sweeting, H. (2004) 'Assisting young people's access to social capital in contemporary families: a qualitative study', *Journal of Youth Studies*, vol 7, no 2, pp 173-90.

Sen, A. (1999) *Development as freedom*, Oxford: Oxford University Press.

Sennett, R. (1999) *The corrosion of character: The personal consequences of work in the new capitalism*, New York, NY: Norton.

Seyd, P. and Whiteley, P. (1992) *Labour's grass roots: The politics of party membership*, Oxford: Clarendon.

Smith, J. and Spurling, A. (1999) *Lifelong learning: Riding the tiger*, London: Cassell/Lifelong Learning Foundation.

Sodexho (2004) *The university lifestyle survey 2004*, London: Sodexho/Times Higher Education Supplement.

Somerville, M. and Abrahamsson, L. (2003) 'Trainers and learners constructing a community of practice: masculine work cultures and learning safety in the mining industry', *Studies in the Education of Adults*, vol 35, no 1, pp 19-34.

Strawn, C. (2002) 'Social capital influences on lifelong learning among adults who didn't finish high school', Adult Education Research Conference, 24-26 May, North Carolina State University.

Strawn, C. (2003) 'The influences of social capital on lifelong learning among adults who did not finish high school', occasional paper, Cambridge, MA: National Centre for the Study of Adult Learning and Literacy.

Swart, J. and Kinnie, N. (2003) 'Sharing knowledge in knowledge intensive firms', *Human Resource Management Journal*, vol 13, no 2, pp 60-74.

Szreter, S. (1999) 'A new political economy for New Labour: the importance of social capital', *Renewal*, vol 7, no 1, pp 30-44.

Szreter, S. (2000) 'Social capital, the economy, and education in historical perspective, in S. Baron, J. Field and T. Schuller (eds) *Social capital: Critical perspectives*, Oxford: Oxford University Press, pp 56-77.

Sztompka, P. (1999) *Trust: A sociological theory*, Cambridge: Cambridge University Press.

Tawney, R. H. (1966) *The radical tradition. Twelve essays on politics, education and literature*, Harmondsworth: Penguin.

Thompson, J. (1983) *Learning liberation: Women's response to men's education*, Beckenham: Croom Helm.

Thorpe, V. (2000) 'What every modern girl needs: a divorce magazine', *Observer*, 3 September, p 5.

Touraine, A. (1995) *Critique of modernity*, Oxford: Blackwell.

TUC (Trades Union Congress) (2004) 'Only one in four non-union workers get regular training', press release 18/5/2004, accessed on 31 May 2005 at www.learningservices.org.uk/national/learning-3706-f0.cfm

Tuckett, A. (2001) *Changing structures, familiar challenges: Annual Report and Accounts 2000-2001*, Leicester: National Institute of Adult Continuing Education, pp 5-10.

Tuijnman, A. and Boudard, E. (2001) *International adult literacy survey: Adult education participation in North America: International perspectives*, Ottawa: Statistics Canada.

Turkle, S. (1997) *Life on the screen: Identity in the age of the internet*, New York, NY: Touchstone.

Uglow, J. (2003) *The lunar men: A story of science, art, invention and passion*, London: Faber and Faber.

Urry, J. (2002) 'Mobility and proximity', *Sociology*, vol 26, no 2, pp 255-74.

Van Laere, K. and Heene, A. (2003) 'Social networks as a source of competitive advantage for the firm', *Journal of Workplace Learning*, vol 15, no 6, pp 248-58.

Vester, M. (1997) 'Soziale Milieus und Individualisierung. Mentalitäten und Konfliktlinien im historischen Wandel', in U. Beck and P. Sopp (eds) *Individualisierung und Integration: neue Konfliktlinien und neuer Integrationsmodus*, Opladen: Leske und Budrich, pp 99-123.

Vester, M. (2005) 'Class and culture in Germany', in F. Devine, M. Savage, J. Scott and R. Crompton (eds) *Rethinking class: Culture, identities and lifestyle*, London: Palgrave Macmillan, pp 69-94.

Vester, M., von Oertzen, P., Geiling, H., Hermann, T. and Müller, D. (2001) *Soziale Milieus im gesellschaftlichen Strukturwandel: Zwischen Integration und Ausgrenzung*, Frankfurt am Main: Suhrkamp.

West, L. (1996) *Beyond fragments: Adults, motivation and higher education – a biographical analysis*, London: Taylor and Francis.

Woolcock, M. (1998) 'Social capital and economic development: toward a theoretical synthesis and policy framework', *Theory and Society*, vol 27, no 2, pp 151-208.

Wright, S. (2001) 'Activating the unemployed: the street-level implementation of UK policy', in J. Clasen (ed) *What future for social policy?*, Dordrecht: Kluwer, pp 235-50.

Young, M. (1998) 'Post-compulsory education for a learning society', in S. Ranson (ed) *Inside the learning society*, London: Cassell.

Zukas, M. and Malcolm, J. (2000) 'Pedagogies for lifelong learning: building bridges or building walls? Supporting lifelong learning: global internet colloquium', accessed on 14 January 2005 at www.open.ac.uk/lifelong-learning/papers

Zwarenstein, M., Atkins, J., Barr, H., Hammick, M., Koppel, I. and Reeves, S. (1999) 'A systematic review of interprofessional education', *Journal of Interprofessional Care*, vol 13, no 4, pp 417-24.

Index

D

E

F

G

H

I

J

K

L